AFTER THE STORM

AFTER THE STORM

Black Intellectuals Explore
the Meaning of
Hurricane Katrina

Edited by David Dante Troutt

THE NEW PRESS

NEW YORK
LONDON

Requests for permission to reproduce selections from this book
should be mailed to: Permissions Department,
The New Press, 38 Greene Street, New York, NY 10013.

Published in the United States by The New Press, New York, 2006
Distributed by W. W. Norton & Company, Inc., New York

LIBRARY OF CONGRESS CATALOGING-IN-PUBLICATION DATA

After the storm : Black intellectuals explore the meaning of Hurricane
Katrina / edited by David Dante Troutt ; with a foreword by Derrick Bell
and an introduction by Charles J. Ogletree Jr.
p. cm.
Includes bibliographical references.
ISBN-13: 978-1-59558-116-7 (hardcover)
ISBN-10: 1-59558-116-2 (hardcover)
1. African Americans—Civil rights—History—21st century.
2. African Americans—Social conditions—21st century.
3. Hurricane Katrina, 2005—Political aspects.   4. Hurricane Katrina,
2005—Social aspects.   5. Racism—Political aspects—United States—
History—21st century.   6. United States—Race relations—
Political aspects—History—21st century.   I. Troutt, David Dante.
E185.615A594 2006
305.896'073076—dc22   2006008883

The New Press was established in 1990 as a not-for-profit alternative to the large, commercial publishing houses currently dominating the book publishing industry. The
New Press operates in the public interest rather than for private gain, and is committed
to publishing, in innovative ways, works of educational, cultural, and community
value that are often deemed insufficiently profitable.

www.thenewpress.com

Composition by dix!
This book was set in Minion

Printed in the United States of America

2   4   6   8   10   9   7   5   3   1

To the many American women, men, and children who called New Orleans and other cities and towns across the Gulf Coast of Louisiana, Mississippi, and Alabama their home on August 29, 2005—the survivors of Hurricane Katrina—and in memory of those who died.

I am not a "refugee." I wasn't shipped here. . . . We are not refugees. You hold your head up. We are United States citizens, and you be proud of that. A lot of us are taxpaying, honest, hardworking people. I'm like, when did I come from another country? That's what they used to call people that was in the boats, and that was sneaking over here. I am a *survivor*. They need to say, "the survivors of Katrina."

—Sharon White, New Orleanian in Baton Rouge shelter,
quoted on National Public Radio's *All Things Considered*,
September 7, 2005

CONTENTS

FOREWORD
Derrick Bell

In the wake of the death and devastation Hurricane Katrina visited on large swaths of Louisiana, Mississippi, and Alabama, it is not surprising that many people asked with some bitterness: "How could a loving God allow this to happen to so many innocent people?"

The question serves to shift attention and responsibility from government officials at every level who ignored specific warnings about the inadequacy of levees, the main defenses against the waters that surround a city perilously perched below sea level. Official derelictions, though, are all too frequent and far less dramatic than swollen bodies floating in flooded streets, homeowners trapped on rooftops awaiting rescue that for many never arrived, and masses of hungry people crowded in the Superdome and the New Orleans Convention Center or stranded on highway overpasses.

Surely, most of Katrina's victims must have prayed for water and food, for shelter, for life. Where then was God? Some fundamentalist preachers, of course, had the answer. Right-wing televangelist, Pat Robertson, always ready with a headline-grabbing biblical proclamation, tied the tragedy to divine wrath for homosexuality and legalized abortion.[1] And a Christian publication surmised with barely suppressed glee that had God not dealt with New Orleans, He would have had to apologize to Sodom and Gomorrah.[2]

Months after the waters receded, when debate about how to rebuild the beleaguered city was under way, New Orleans mayor C. Ray Nagin told a Martin Luther King Jr. Day celebration that "as we think about rebuilding New Orleans, surely God is mad at America. He's sending hurricane after hurricane. And it's destroying, it's putting stress on this country." Nagin suggested that God retaliated against New Orleans because He did not approve "of us being in Iraq under false pretenses. But surely," the mayor continued, "He's upset at black America also. We're not taking care of ourselves. We're not taking care of our women. And we're not taking care of our children."[3]

These few instances reflect what almost always happens when things go very wrong; the blame for Hurricane Katrina's monumental destruction was placed on God. Either he had wreaked vengeance on good and bad alike as retaliation for some human wrongdoing, or, busy elsewhere, he had failed to respond to the prayers and supplications of even the righteous.

Contributors to this volume were too moved by the Katrina experience either to blame God or to plead ignorance about the continuing burdens of prejudice based on color and economic condition that belie the general view that racism is history. We are all too aware of the history of systemic discrimination, altering in form but always debilitating in effect, that rendered residents of New Orleans's Ninth Ward as vulnerable to Katrina's high winds and collapsed levees as they have been to low-paying jobs, high rents and mortgages, inadequate police protection, underfunded schools, and poor to nonexistent social services.

Even so, the suffering caused by Katrina, the snail's pace of rescue and recovery efforts, and the not so subtle plans to bar from return those who with their forebears had made New Orleans New Orleans, served as an epiphany for us who thought we knew. Whites as well as blacks lost much to the winds and floods of Katrina, but for black people, the deadly drama of the experience marked an official close to civil rights era dreams of equality of opportunity, if not social acceptance. Through the lens, not of Katrina, but of the response to Katrina, we now know beyond denying that while things are not now what they once were, the reforms, progress if you will, are more surface than substance. That surface is like gossamer, evanescent and easily dispelled when policymakers' interests are drawn elsewhere, usually to the attractions of money and power.

Amid the shambles of our hopes upon which we have relied much and worked long, the writers here strive to understand, to seek new, firmer foundations in a society still ready to utilize our achievements while rejecting in ways, both overt and subtle, the achievers. What counsel can we offer in a period that so resembles the late 1870s? Then, support for Reconstruction—despite the herculean efforts of our forebears—was being sacrificed for political gains that were more important than the rights, liberties, even lives, of those so recently freed from a most cruel and abject bondage.

In seeking that counsel for ourselves as well as others, is there a place for God as we seek something in life beyond mere existence and hopeless endurance? I think that there is a basis on which to build. When the "where was God" question was posed to Rabbi Michael Lerner following the 2004 tsunami that killed more than three hundred thousand people, he responded, "Isn't this an attempt to avoid the more pressing question of 'Where was humanity?' Why have we been so unwilling to take serious responsibility for the well-being of others on the planet?"[4]

In fact, when the media gave broad coverage to the devastation caused by the tsunami and Hurricane Katrina, humanity did respond. Having seen the photographs of distress and read the stories, humanity reached out with dollars, with clothing, with volunteers from across the country who went at their own expense to the disaster centers, offering their skills, the comfort of their presence. Such an outpouring of aid and sympathy for strangers proves that just below the surface, there is good that the horror of sudden death and loss brings out.

The challenge is to find a basis for empathy and support that is not directly linked to a natural disaster or something deemed, as the insurance companies put it, an "act of God." Explanations for inaction come easily. Most of us are more than occupied with caring for self, family, and relatives, those to whom we are—like it or not—closely connected. For reasons so deeply ingrained that they defy easy description, race somehow insulates people of color from the empathy of active concern more readily extended to whites. At least in part, this insensitivity is a by-product of a competitive system that not so quietly urges us to get ahead of others by any means we can imagine. Success is rewarded, even glorified, no matter how it is attained.

Yet, we know that economic and political decisions cause far more suffering than even the worst natural disaster. Without the excuse providing or God blaming hurricanes, tornadoes, raging fires, and swiftly rising floodwaters, thousands are constantly threatened by forces beyond their control, not simply poverty and prejudice, but economic dislocations—outsourcing of jobs, closing of plants, downsizing of staff—that each year plunge thousands of the comfortably employed middle class into the growing ranks of the needy, threatened with foreclosure of their homes, burdened with credit card debt.

How can we awaken that sense of humanity within us that some call God to address the needs of those whose plight is the fault of man, not God? Perhaps, as many theologians think, we should view God not as a superbeing somewhere up there who determines our fates and can, at will, intervene in our lives. Rather, as the Reverend Forrest Church suggests, we can strengthen our determination by viewing God as a "co-creator with us in an unfolding, intricate drama of hitherto unimaginable complexity." We are not simply "actors on God's stage, by this reading of creation history, we are participants in the scripting of God's drama."[5]

Something like this concept, whatever it is called, is needed to move us beyond our present understanding, which, if we are honest, provokes the opposite of optimism. The task before us is not easy and may not be achievable. Despair and fatalism, though, were not the option of those forebears whose prospects for the future were no worse than ours. Encouraged by their survival and growth, we can emulate the commitment of the slave singer who wrote the lyric: "I will go; I shall go, to see what the end will be."

Derrick Bell
April 2006

NOTES

1. "Religious Conservatives Claim Katrina Was God's Omen, Punishment for the United States," Media Matters for Americans, September 13, 2005, http://mediamatters.org/items/200509130004.

2. "A Purity Comes to New Orleans," *Christian Voice*, September 13, 2005, http://www.christianvoice.org.uk/Press/press010.html.

3. Miguel Bustillo, "A Hurricane May Be God's Punishment, Mayor Says," *Los Angeles Times*, January 17, 2006. A few days later, the mayor apologized, deeming his statement totally inappropriate.

4. Rabbi Michael Lerner, "God, the Tsunami, and Human Generosity," *Tikkun*, January 2, 2005.

5. Forrest Church, "Acts of God," a sermon delivered at the All Souls Church on January 9, 2005.

ACKNOWLEDGMENTS

I am grateful to all my thoughtful colleagues in and outside the academy who dedicated themselves to this swift undertaking. These busy contributors bent time to produce essays and analyses of the finest quality. I am indebted to their efforts.

This collection would not have been possible without Diane Wachtell's almost instant recognition of what we hoped to accomplish and her unflagging support along the way. It was a pleasure to work with her again and benefit from her warm acumen. A variety of constraints made this a difficult endeavor, and Diane and her staff at The New Press often found ways to make it easier. In particular, Joel Ariaratnam moved boulders with clever grace.

I am extremely grateful for the tireless research assistance of Dennis Kim-Prieto at the Rutgers-Newark Law School library as well as the short-notice heroics of my research assistant, Shermona Mapp. My research in the city of New Orleans would have been no more than a long, sad walk without the productive interventions of my dear friend Keith Coleman. I was also helped in the project by Janet Dewart Bell, Maritza Braswell, Erica Campbell, and Alanah E. Odoms.

As always, I owe unspeakable amounts of love, devotion, and deepest gratitude to my strong and insightful wife, Shawn Dawson Troutt, and my indomitable daughter and sweet superhero, Naima Vary Troutt, for their support and ready humor. None of my efforts are possible without the brilliant example of my mother, Dr. Bobbye Vary Troutt, in whose memory all my hard work is reflected.

David Dante Troutt
Brooklyn, New York

INTRODUCTION
Charles J. Ogletree Jr.

New Orleans is vitality and culture. It is the city of the blues, beignets, and Bourbon Street. It is the city of grits in the morning, gumbo at noon, and, for those so moved, gambling from sunrise to sunrise. It is a city where young black boys tap-dance for tips, and see drunken college students roam the streets of the French Quarter, taking advantage of the many clubs that allow drinking well into the night, without any sense of moderation.

New Orleans is a city where the Essence Music Festival, perhaps the largest annual gathering of African Americans, occurs every July. Because it is a party with a purpose, one could spend the morning attending various workshops on black self-esteem, debate issues of personal responsibility, and have an opportunity to meet and greet some of the nation's most prominent African American authors during book signings. As the day turned to night, New Orleans life took on another flavor, as thousands would spend the evening enjoying the timeless old-school talent of the O'Jays, the svelte voice of Luther Vandross, or even the new generation of artists like Mary J. Blige and John Legend. But the Essence

Music Festival was always capped, as it should be, by the sultry sound of Frankie Beverly and Maze belting out their classic, "Happy People."

The New Orleans of yesterday conjures images of joy, excitement, and celebration, a picture that underscores the vivaciousness of this great city. Indeed, New Orleans is a city where even a funeral is a celebration of life, with bands marching through the streets, reminding people of that purpose, and where graveyards are aboveground a powerful symbol of the people of New Orleans, and yet a reminder that New Orleans is below sea level.

The New Orleans we have known and loved for so long may never be the same; the crumbling levees transformed it on August 29, 2005. From that moment forward, we have been faced with the question of whether or not the great city, which is unlike any other in the United States, where there is no end to the night, where revelers enjoy Mardi Gras, where women will display their breasts for a few beads, and where people shake off all of their inhibitions, will *ever* return.

The essays in this book dig broadly and deeply, trying to discover the old New Orleans, and offering critical analyses of whether there will be a *new* New Orleans. They explore the issue in all of its majesty and grace, with all of its pain and contradictions, and with the ambiguities that make one wonder whether the great city that we all knew and loved will ever exist again.

The real question posed by New Orleans is more than whether it will ever rise above the ashes, the floods, and the pain of 2005. Indeed, the harder question is whether it *should*. That question is particularly hard because, as this collection of essays makes clear, the issue of race is deeply connected to the issue of survival. Foreign photographers captured the dilemma of race in this great city as it played out during Hurricane Katrina. During the height of the flood, as New Orleans residents struggled to survive in desperate circumstances, a young white couple entered an abandoned grocery store and reportedly found food; meanwhile, the caption of another photograph taken around the same time describes an African American male as looting from an abandoned store. It is not the simple views of the media that matter; it is the perception of race in the city of New Orleans, and the state of Louisiana, and the United States of America that should concern us. It is a perplexing and painful topic, and one that may deeply influence whether or not New Orleans will rise again.

Prior to Katrina, New Orleans had a somewhat vibrant economy and was a popular destination for tourists from around the world. People loved the food, the music, and the southern hospitality. What they did not see and what was never visible was the devastating poverty and despair that were within a stone's throw of Bourbon Street and the French Quarter. Those who came to New Orleans to revel in the culture never traveled to the Ninth Ward. They never saw the pervasive poverty that defined life in New Orleans for so many residents there. They never had to imagine how thousands of people, without resources, cars, or connections, might be trapped in the event of an emergency.

While tens of thousands of African Americans from around the country would travel to the Superdome and sway to the great music every July, they never had to worry about whether the bathrooms worked, whether the hurricane would cause the roof to collapse, or whether their lives would be threatened in this environment of strangers brought together because of the crisis that the city faced in the summer of 2005.

The two faces of New Orleans remind us that we have unfinished business to do in thinking about how race matters in America. The more perplexing problem that is evident from this collection of outstanding essays is what will emerge in 2006.

What one must worry about is the likelihood that as the devastation in New Orleans, as well as in Alabama, Florida, and Mississippi, is no longer front-page news, the displacement of thousands of New Orleans's citizens will simply become a footnote in history. Those who offered open arms at the beginning of this American natural disaster have pulled away their helping hands. There is no longer the cry to send around the country, to paraphrase Emma Lazarus, our "sick, our tired, our poor, huddled masses yearning to breathe free." The reaction has been a pervasive one, and a rejection of the idea of comforting and supporting those who have suffered so much in New Orleans.

Indeed, the backlash against the citizens of New Orleans is terrifying. In the beginning, the survivors were received with enthusiastic welcomes. However, months later the children of New Orleans find themselves the victims of constant threats, harassment, and even physical abuse in the public schools in Houston. They have overstayed their welcome, and they are becoming targets of violence and hate.

The academic institutions that hastily created programs to accept students are also retreating. Schools from Stanford University to Harvard University, from Howard University to Brown University, have opened their doors to admit students to continue their education. It is a compelling and honorable thing that was done. Nevertheless, for those students from New Orleans whose opportunities to study at home were diminished, the open doors for them as guests have slowly begun to close. Indeed, the *Harvard Crimson,* several weeks after warmly welcoming students from

New Orleans colleges, editorialized that this should be a temporary, as opposed to a permanent, measure:

> Visiting students who wish to transfer to Harvard permanently and those who support that proposal should realize that it is unfair to the hurricane-affected schools who explicitly expressed in conjunction with Harvard that students would be required to return once the fall semester ended. They should understand that dishonoring that contract would set a negative precedent for any future such actions in response to hurricane-affected or disaster-affected areas.[1]

Furthermore, there are signs that the New Orleans that we once knew will never be the same. Indeed, the idea of developing New Orleans as a site for lucrative business opportunities may overshadow the idea of returning the displaced and overwhelmed residents back to their homes in the future.

The possibility that New Orleans must really confront, and one that deeply worries me, is that the Donald Trumps and Donald Ducks, real estate developers and entertainment entities, will find serious revenue streams available in the *new* New Orleans, while public housing, quality education, and an infrastructure that provides health care and employment are no longer of greatest concern.

As we think about the impact of Katrina on New Orleans in particular, it is possible that the black community we knew may never exist again. This book is designed to make us critically examine that possible impact, to anticipate the difficulties that lie ahead, and to ensure that the tragic losses from August 2005, as well as the destruction and devastation that were witnessed, do not become an excuse to ignore a community that so desperately needs leadership, compassion, and protection.

What we ultimately learn from these essays concerning Katrina and its aftermath is that the manner in which we portray those harmed is profoundly important, and potentially determinative of whether we will address the disaster's broader implications. This incisive collection of essays compellingly reminds us that portrayals of the Katrina tragedy for black Americans involve many factors on multiple fronts. The realities are complex, and often contradictory. The idea of portrayal assumes, perhaps erroneously, visibility. Several authors provide insight into the theme of visibility and invisibility, especially for the vast numbers of black poor in New Orleans. To what extent has the devastation and failure to help the Ninth Ward and other low-income, minority areas been highlighted or ignored? To what extent have people in America seen the black poor as victims? As problems? How are these realities portrayed?

The first two essays explore the historic creation of ghetto neighborhoods in cities like New Orleans to highlight the tragic nexus of race and class when Katrina struck. David Troutt's narrative focuses the city's rebuilding efforts on the persistently poor residents displaced by generations of vulnerability and months of official neglect. Ultimately, he sees the failures as deeply embedded in American social and political culture and the solutions as matters of affirming our social contract. Sheryll Cashin also writes about how Katrina demonstrates the physical organization of the American metropolis and how that organization has shaped our race relations. One of the greatest challenges to recovery, she asserts, is to acknowledge the hypersegregation that preexisted the storm and to dismantle it in favor of communities where middle-class norms may take root.

Politics—and especially racial politics—is the central theme of

the two essays in Part Two. John Valery White covers an astonish-
ing range of the political terrain in New Orleans and Louisiana
leading up to the storm. His analysis demonstrates how, despite
well-publicized fears of a New Orleans purged of its black majority
population, long-standing contradictions and interdependencies
in the region's politics make that unlikely. Adolph Reed's essay attacks the emphasis on racial inequality in any analysis of Katrina,
favoring instead political analyses that demonstrate the common
points of suffering among vulnerable people across the country.
Race, and especially racism, Reed argues, is not a language capable
of directing change.

In Part Three, we see the disaster and the diaspora it engendered
in critical historical relief. In his brief introduction to the section,
historian Clement Price reminds readers of the close link between
natural disaster and black migrations in American history, and
suggests that Katrina may be extraordinary only in a contemporary social and economic context. Michael Eric Dyson's tour-de-
force is both analysis of that historical context and call-to-action
for the present diaspora of displaced blacks. Historically, he argues, migrations have been submerged, subversive, and subsidized. Katrina has been at least all three for blacks, a complicated
sum of factors that has not only increased pains and hardships but
the challenges to recovery for the displaced in their new homes.
The story as it unfolds may be as much about their resourcefulness
as it is the story of the nation.

Katrina revealed a lot about racial perception in America, as few
events have. Part Four examines racial identity through the meanings fixed upon Katrina by the media and popular discourse.
Devon Carbado and Cheryl Harris deconstruct the "frames"
through which facts about the disaster were filtered. They show

that the work of antiracism may require much more than simply bringing better facts to bear. Perception is deeper. Katheryn Russell-Brown takes up similar notions of what the public saw in New Orleans. Using the idea of "a-justice" (the failure of law to operate as a means to do justice), she details many harms committed against New Orleanians that could and should be considered criminal acts.

The idea that there ought to be some body of law somewhere that could be invoked to vindicate some of the wrongs committed against Katrina's survivors is raised again in Adrien Wing's essay. She compares what is happening to survivors with claims that might be brought under the international law principles of treaties binding upon the United States. Yet Anthony Farley's stunning essay—a prose poem finale—will have none of it. Beginning with the forgotten question of why the Amtrak trains would not move to evacuate New Orleanians, he takes readers on a journey back to slavery and the markings of inferiority that began with that institution and were again revealed by Katrina. Only mutual aid, he concludes, will remove the stain.

Ultimately, fruitful tensions develop in these pages as the authors struggle with the difficult task of determining how race should be portrayed in post-Katrina efforts to rebuild. We are appropriately cautioned about the risk of portraying black victims of Katrina as losers, and the consequences of drawing such conclusions. We are reminded, as we read these sobering accounts, of the risks associated with identifying injustices while trying to avoid fueling stereotypes. We are cautioned as well about the double-edged sword of over- or understating the significance of race in analyzing what went horribly wrong, and why the response was handled in such a shockingly cavalier fashion.

Through all the writings, there is a sense that the portrayal of and response to Katrina are important for more than just this specific moment in time. The New Orleans we have known has vanished, and we no longer have the luxury of acting like tourists, disregarding the poverty in favor of gumbo and gambling, all the while believing that we were *all* Happy People. Katrina presents an opportunity to develop a model for future disaster response. However, this model must not forget the roles of race and class in its portrayal and framework of reality. A model that ignores the visibility of the marginalized and disenfranchised perpetuates the reasons behind response failures for Katrina. This is a timely book, and its message is one that should generate debate, reform, and a deeper appreciation of how race can often complicate our attention to matters of national concern.

NOTES

1. *Harvard Crimson,* December 5, 2005.

Part One

RACE, POVERTY, AND PLACE

MANY THOUSANDS GONE, AGAIN
David Dante Troutt

Anyone who has experienced sudden death close up knows that it need not be instantaneous, but may take all day. The grief that follows is a little more stunning than for anticipated deaths, and the understanding of how to go on is as elusive as the lingering doubts about the unspoken good-bye. Survivors often blame themselves or, worse, descend into a limbo that can stretch on for years. And if the limbo is compounded by acts of willful indifference or rumors about mythical depravity by those just outside the sudden death, a loss might never be overcome. That limbo may become the intertwined fate of the lost and her survivors, the condition of feeling eternally blamed.

The city of New Orleans presented innumerable images of its sudden deaths in the aftermath of Hurricane Katrina, but none was more memorable to me than the sight of a blackened swath of flooded street and, off to the right, a sliver of dry highway overpass. Surrounded by ringlets of raindrops, the bloated body of a black woman shrouded in white lies facedown and adrift in the water. The humiliation of her death is added to only slightly by an embarrassing stain near her anus. Several feet to the right of the corpse is a full black plastic garbage bag. To the right of that, life continues again in the form of a large black woman, bending to pour water for a despondent-looking pit bull, both safe on the overpass.

Death was sudden for the corpse in the street. She may have fought off a fast-filling living room and struggled a long while before giving out. She may have floated down familiar blocks or merely dropped in her tracks short of some goal. Her death seems to reflect the special vulnerability black women faced against the rising waters; the slow rescues; the total disappearance of privacy, sustenance, and protection; many with children beside them, many others elderly. She is a warning to the woman with the dog. All we know for sure is that she was a human being, almost certainly poor, desperate, and dishonorably unknown at her nightmarish end—except by those who loved her. We must assume that she, like each of the hundreds destroyed by Katrina's horror, was loved despite the overwhelming evidence to the contrary. Our gut tells us that only the most despised soul could be left like that. Thanks to the camera lens, she drowns forever in sympathy. Most Americans, moved by shame, would have attended her funeral.

As we struggle to make useful sense of what happened so that the lives that continue are not forever diminished by devastation, we know that the woman on the overpass also suffered sudden loss—most likely her home, a job, institutional relationships with familiar actors, and so forth. With the dispersal of her friends and family, she lost reasonable expectations about how tomorrows get handled. In that snapshot before her evacuation, there was no telling in which of forty-four states FEMA would decide to drop her. For the many thousands gone from New Orleans, most for the first time, the disorientation about an unfathomable future may be as crippling as the heartache of a lost past. This is true for a great number of exiled New Orleanians—white, Asian, Latino, and black—including many middle-class and affluent people whose faces never made the news. Katrina was a perfect storm in many respects, colluding with numerous known and unknown pressure points to produce an array of destruction unimaginable in a developed country.

However, what somehow made the news—those images of sweltering black bodies clamoring to survive in the Superdome and the convention center, to board a bus, to make it safely through chest-high water, to reunite with babies and husbands and mothers—was probably the world's last look at an urban way of life. What comes back, who, and how, is the hard work of a grief unique for the scope of its challenges. Disasters happen. They regularly expose the vulnerability of poor people in substandard housing. And the experts all agree that disaster was due for the poor people of New Orleans, even though, as former mayor Sidney Barthelemy explained, Gulf hurricanes "usually curve off." Because this one didn't curve off in time, the science of storms and ecosystems met the dynamics of race, space, and marginalization in a generation's single most profound spectacle of cumulative black disadvantage. The combination of institutionalized injustices, real bad luck, and stunningly incompetent disaster relief heaped relentless hardships on a fragile diaspora of households too used to how stress and hardship beget the same. Then they were called out of their names, accused in the press of shooting at their own rescuers, looting their own survival, defamed for rapes that never occurred, ignored for the rapes that did, and in a mythologizing process that is still unfolding, blamed for their own need.

The reconstruction, therefore, should begin with them. Though rarely tried it is nevertheless true about the social contract that what benefits the poorest members of a community usually benefits us all. Reconstruction should begin with a recognition that what cruel intention and criminal negligence did to the black poor in New Orleans before and up to the final evacuation is the symbolic crucible of what America has done to most cities east of the Mississippi with large black populations since at least World War II. And it should end with an equally spectacular effort to remake the American social contract.

AMERICANIZING CITIES

The New Orleans historian and urbanist Arnold Hirsch uses the term "Americanization" to describe how the city's white Creoles gradually relinquished the distinct ethnic identity that had helped make New Orleans a metropolis characterized by at least three racial tiers, rather than the two, black and white, that have dominated the social and political realities of most American cities.[1] Creole capitulation into a blander, more homogenous American white affiliation, he suggests, helped to diminish the social incentives for the city's historic integration and instead promoted a segregated social fabric. In return, white Creoles joined segregation's privileged, and the city constructed racial advantages and disadvantages across the urban landscape. In other words, racial dualism facilitated racialized spaces. The seeds of this process were germinating around the middle of the last century, always threatening to transform a truly unique American city—a monument to slavery, trade, reconciliation, resistance, and cultural admixture—into a mere exotic example of the familiar pattern of the urban binary. In the name of assimilation, some version of this submission to whiteness by a white ethnic group was performed continuously across northeastern cities by European immigrants bargaining for similar advantages. Now, after Katrina's massive ground clearance, the devolution away from the hope of something truly interesting and radically beautiful among American cities may give way to the latest commodified form: Disney on the Mississippi. In the unspoken terms of this consumption fest, a poor (black, Democratic) population that can be jettisoned, must be jettisoned for the sake of new subdivisions, better schools, and lower taxes. Hence, anything that slows their return to New Orleans is an obvious benefit; and nothing slows like absolute limbo.

With a different focus but just as prescient, the sociologist William Julius Wilson's descriptions of the social effects of post-industrial urban decline provide a structuralist prophecy of New Orleans's fate. At first blush, Wilson's analysis would appear misplaced; New Orleans is a port and commercial economy, not a center of industrial manufacturing. Yet the hurricane's ruins reveal more similarities to Cleveland, Chicago, and Philadelphia than differences. Wilson asserted that the primary effect of federal housing policy, white flight, urban depopulation, and the rise of a low-wage service economy is a deepening isolation and concentration of the urban (particularly black) poor.[2] No longer necessary to a manufacturing sector that generally paid workers well enough to cover mortgages and provide pensions, college tuition, and other facets of middle-class existence, these folk became irrelevant.[3] As their social distance from mainstream life increased with each generation, they grew more culturally distinct (gangster rap); incarceratable (prison industrial complex); unassimilable (Ebonics); pathological (out-of-wedlock birth, infant mortality, and low "marriageability" rates); labelable ("underclass," "looters," "playas," "hoes," "pimps"); and detestable. Wilson might disagree with some of the latter characterization, preferring to focus on their rates of joblessness or labor force nonparticipation. For example, in New Orleans, 44 percent of all black men sixteen and older were jobless before Hurricane Katrina struck.[4] Wilson also downplayed the significance of race as a reliable factor in explaining this portrait of the urban persistently poor. It's not worth the quarrel except to say that a special kind of hatred has consistently manifested itself in the American psyche, and it is as undeniably present in this pattern of economic marginalization as in the face-down shame of the corpse floating down a New Orleans street.

Yet before it was race *and* class, as the post-Katrina news reports insisted, it was unarguably race. New Orleans's blacks were relegated to a lower status and lower ground by the same fixtures of white American economic advantage at work in most cities after slavery: Jim Crow laws preventing access to business opportunities and home ownership, de facto and de jure segregation rules, restrictive covenants, mob violence, blatant race discrimination in mortgage-lending criteria, and, of course, nearly total political disenfranchisement until roughly fifty years ago. These structures of racist intention helped forge the city's landscape even during the prewar years, when New Orleans enjoyed a reputation as a fairly integrated city. Pontchartrain Park, for example, was among the first middle-class enclaves available to black doctors and lawyers and teachers, built (on low ground) in 1950. It was remarkable both for the existence of a black population to settle it and for the white population that allowed it. Today, however, intentional racial discrimination against blacks persists in housing and employment.[5]

The federal government had a special hand in instilling vulnerability among New Orleans's black population, just as it had in cities across the country. Public housing projects were racially segregated from their inception in 1937, when the Housing Authority of New Orleans became the first agency of its kind to receive federal funds.[6] As elsewhere, the siting of public housing projects in New Orleans was often cruel and surgical, carving away integrated neighborhoods or areas with a thriving black working- and middle-class infrastructure.[7] During World War II, these were not yet forbidden places. However, they became so in the war's aftermath, especially in the 1950s, when demand among lower-income black families increased and white families moved on to better opportunities in what would become more stable, overwhelmingly white suburbs. When the 1949 federal housing law offered more funds for housing, New Orleans chose to expand existing projects.[8] When those communities began to decline under the weight of an increasingly poor population and a diminishing city tax base, due in part to white flight and drugs, ghettoization got going in earnest. Ghettos are not easily undone.

Yet, with the aid of federal highway funds for critical arteries such as U.S. 61 and Interstate 10, ghettos became easier to flee. Suburban sprawl is now the dominant form of residential organization in the country, the truest expression of Americanization in an idealistic sense. The federal government assisted its random development in New Orleans with roads as well as flood protection. It is clear by now that the negligence of the Army Corps of Engineers probably hastened the flood that killed more than a thousand New Orleanians and destroyed more than two hundred thousand homes. Many suburbs were built on wetlands and marshes, exchanging ecological balance for draining technology in a gamble that always raised the stakes for the poorest people in the region.[9] Engineering reallocated flood risks to lower, cheaper land by removing environmental buffers and encouraging development of subdivisions. Bullheaded federal endorsement of these trends is demonstrated by the fact that over the last quarter century Orleans and Jefferson parishes represented 20 percent of the entire nation's property claims for *repeat losses* paid by the National Flood Insurance Program.[10]

This is why one may never talk honestly about the American ideal of middle-class life without talking about its antithesis in ghettos. The one made the other and historically depended on it for its existence. By September 2005, nowhere were the abusive effects of this codependent relationship more obvious than New Orleans. Some numbers about the segregated topography of unequal burdens bear this out. Of the households living in the flooded areas of Orleans Parish (the city), 80 percent were black.[11] The average annual income of households in flooded areas was about $38,000 compared with $55,000 for those in nonflooded areas.[12] The homeownership rate in flooded areas was 53 percent compared with 69 percent in nonflooded areas.[13] Half the flood victims were renters. Fifty thousand children were displaced by Katrina's waters. Half of them had only a single parent to help reconstruct their lives.[14] And where lives are perhaps hardest and most tenuous for families with children—public housing—the New Orleans population was 100 percent black.[15] Most projects are located in areas of "extreme poverty" (i.e., those in which *at least* 40 percent of all households have incomes below the official poverty threshold). In 2000, New Orleans had forty-seven extremely poor census tracts. Katrina inundated thirty-eight of them.[16] In a city built on environmental risk, poor blacks were literally kept low down until they became irrelevant.

Wilson was right about New Orleans. The period between 1970 and 2000 saw the Americanization of that city's periphery and the consolidation of urban hardships. Never the manufacturing hub, New Orleans still lost 13,500 good jobs during that period, while low-paying service and retail employment grew by 136 percent and 76 percent, respectively.[17] Half the city's white population left in that span of time, mostly for the surrounding areas.[18] This familiar trend in economic and political decentralization stimulated the employment base in surrounding St. Tammany, Jefferson, and St. Charles parishes, creating a spatial mismatch between city residents and gainful work. Suburban folks needed cars to traverse the distances that grew with the 25 percent increase in the metropolitan area's urbanized land over the last twenty-five years.[19] And with only a couple days' warning last August, hundreds of thousands of them—the vast majority—got into those cars and got away from New Orleans again. In the city's flooded areas, by contrast, a third lacked automobile access, including about half of all poor black residents and half of all those kids and elderly people.[20]

THE VILLAGE

By the time I finally reached the city one hundred days after the storm, the population was back up to one hundred thousand or so, but the place still resembled the neutron bomb scares of my youth in which those materialistic Russians, we were told, would kill us with weapons that would leave our precious cities intact. I drove and drove, occasionally I walked, but almost nowhere stirred a living soul. The sheer magnitude of a brutalized city that goes on for more miles than it should was breathtaking. I was a voyeur to a civilization whose people now seemed extinct. For all the talk of the

Lower Ninth Ward—and it was jaw-droppingly awful—the neighborhood known as B.W. Cooper offered a less obvious vision of the feared Negro Removal. A place of barren, hideous, and stupidly spaced housing projects within walking distance of downtown, B.W. Cooper had a 70 percent poverty rate in 2000.[21] Only 4 percent of its households owned their own homes compared with 60 percent in the Lower Ninth Ward. In the Lower Ninth, average household income was twice the $13,786 in B.W. Cooper. To be certain, with over a third of its population living below poverty (and many, many more struggling close to it), the Lower Ninth was a poor (but historically proud and important) neighborhood. B.W. Cooper resembles a wasteland, a Bantustan, the type of sad and dangerous place that only malevolent housing policies and public contempt could design. And I walked freely through it without looking over my shoulder once.[22]

The initial catastrophe inspired me to desperate but quaint hopes for a model recovery, including the idea of what a village would do. If New Orleans had been a small town or rural village savaged by nature, I imagined, the community would have come together with all its resources, its grief, and, perhaps through the wisdom of elders, put a recovery plan to work. There would be a role for every villager, down to the youngest, meaning that by the time years later when the homes and businesses and roads were rebuilt, there would be a deeper understanding of how things worked, a personal appreciation of the origins and goals of institutions, a collective pride of ownership, and, of course, a whole lot of people skilled in the work of community building. For this quaint idea to have any application to New Orleans, the survivors would have to have a means to get good information, and they could not stay gone too long.

The reality of New Orleans quickly undermined these assumptions and shed doubt on the sweet hope of a village. On Seventh Street where the block opens to meet the aboveground cemetery, Ms. Hendricks had just returned that day from exile in Memphis and stood alone on her tiny front lawn. At least seventy years old, probably older, she was an elder of the city, having arrived from Greenwood, Mississippi, when she was just thirteen. She never imagined being elsewhere. This was her home, she said. It was not clear what prompted her to come back when she did, since she got no better information than the news reports on TV. Though she was polite to me, Ms. Hendricks kept putting a dark hand to her lips and scanning the street, her full cheekbones squinting in a look of question. Mayor Nagin was the "president" until I reminded her otherwise. She showed me the peeling wood panels on the side of her brick-front shotgun shack, said she was glad there was no mold inside but didn't know how much damage she'd sustained. Understandably, Ms. Hendricks seemed deeply confused. She looked about for neighbors to talk to, but there was only one, a man, who was busy moving belongings into his car.

Yet for another New Orleanian I met moments later, Christopher, there was anything but confusion. White, gay, and no more than twenty-five, this city native and budding real estate agent was making more money than he or the other white realtors nearby in the Garden District had ever imagined. He admitted to never having been in Ms. Hendricks's neighborhood, though it is only eight or nine blocks away. Here, at the realty where Christopher works, the cemetery is separated from the immaculate streets not by mesh fencing but by grand stucco walls. The FEMA workers snap up any rentals available with their $250 housing per diem, including his own apartment, Christopher explained. He fielded daily calls from speculators in California trying to buy up condos in the Ware-house District. Then he drew me a map of the fertile real estate crescent within the larger Crescent City—a shrewd grin inside an embarrassed smile. This was land the river protected, he added. Prices only increased after the storm, often within days. New Orleans wasn't going anywhere.

No, but Ms. Hendricks will. Without a village sensibility, a reli-able means of reaching exiled residents in the cause of meaningful participation, and a protective purpose to preempt greed, she and her neighbors in their conveniently located pocket of poverty will be bought out by speculators acting much faster than slow-footed and deliberately recalcitrant insurance companies (signs every-where scream: "Will Pay CASH for Your Home!"). Eventually, with few family members or friends to anchor her, she will be swept out on a gentrifying storm, and Christopher will learn this area at last.

Though a loose collection of abandoned neighborhoods, the sprawling city itself was no village. I ventured way out along I-10 to New Orleans East, as Mayor Barthelemy had counseled, to see what he called the black middle class's "equity in America." New Orleans East is so far from, say, the concentrated poverty camp of B.W. Cooper's empty shells that it is hard to imagine it is still part of the city or within the storm's reach. New Orleans East is familiar to black middle-class people throughout the country. I found the same winding, suburban-looking streets with ranch homes on quarter-acre lots that stand on Eight Mile near Detroit or Baldwin Hills in L.A. Crowder is the same commercial thoroughfare with the same assortment of banks, strip malls, restaurant chains, and gas stations you see everywhere. Nothing about it suggests a partic-ular race anymore. But I was told that black folks lived in these houses, one after another as far as the eye could see, now gutted neatly down to the studs. And the few nonworkmen who drove up to a house or stood scratching their heads in front of one were indeed black.

The former mayor, cream colored and stately with wavy white hair, who as the city's second black top official served two terms beginning in 1986, was almost tearful about this part of town. They will lose their equity, their life's work, he explained, "for Iraq." New Orleans East was completely submerged because of wave topping and storm surges off Lake Pontchartrain, not because a levee broke. The federal government will not assure homeowners that it will spend the money necessary to construct a system capable of withstanding a category 5 hurricane or similar flood protection even though the Corps' poor engineering created this risk in the first place. The money's all going to fight the useless war in Iraq, Barthelemy believes. And so there can be no village to support the middle-class lives wrenched from New Orleans's historic cauldron of racial checkmates, economic sideswiping, raw deals, and now bad luck. Without patients doctors lose practices, without students teachers lose classrooms, without clients lawyers lose businesses, and so on. The prospects look a lot like nightfall here. The workmen go home and there is not an electrical current alive along the commercial strip or the blocks lined with homes. The place becomes a desert wilderness, the only light coming from the window of one of a few lonely white trailers sitting on lawns. Inside, a homeowner who has dared to return plans her next move or holds on in steadfast defiance of limbo.

Anybody would want to come home again. Nobody wants to be forced out of his or her familiar by violent fate. And a good way to respond to sudden death is to resume bit by bit the work of normalcy, to return from the exile of grief. This is especially true for the citizens of New Orleans, who more than in the vast majority of metropolitan communities never left theirs before, or for long. They have an uncanny sense of local affiliation. Yet they bear another trait that severely complicates this impulse to return: they are close-knit. In America, it is easier to imagine victims of disaster recovering with atomistic resourcefulness, picking up their spouse and two kids and relocating to new opportunity. Americans may even expect that, or at least consider it the rational thing to do. But New Orleanians disproportionately lived near family and extended family, in neighborhoods and with neighbors that provided years of incalculable support and probably a different sense of normalcy than American consumers seek out. They are old-school. Which makes the decision to return, stay in Houston, or find some other place doubly and triply complicated. I tried to imagine how difficult it must have been for a typical New Orleanian family to hold a simple funeral for a dead elder a month after Katrina. There are so many factors. So many people who can't be forgotten.

This brings me back to the not-so-quaint notion of the village. Why, I asked a developer with leadership ties to Mayor Nagin, hasn't Katrina been viewed as a millennial opportunity to employ hundreds, if not thousands, of jobless and unskilled black New Orleanians in demolition and construction—good jobs, good skills training, and great prospects for a city that will be rebuilding for at least another decade? Why didn't the mayor reach out right away and seize upon construction-related work for his displaced, poor constituents? Two reasons, she explained sympathetically. First, the tasks have been overwhelming for all involved. After September 11, for instance, New York mayor Rudy Giuliani could focus on a concentrated piece of land while most services, housing, and essential personnel remained available and intact; the national economy was still flush and we were not at war. In contrast, Nagin faced a city under noxious salt water, his own home destroyed. Second, there wasn't enough temporary housing for indigenous workers and their families in high-ground areas nearby—that is, in predominantly white middle-class parishes.

I concede the first reason. Yet, in light of the enormity of the loss to the city and its desperate residents (as well as the inequitable benefits to out-of-state contractors who could as easily build temporary housing as anything else), I resist the second. It would be a fight, but in an emergency the city (with state help) has to get that land.

Katrina represented a critical moment for black political leadership, a chance to step forward and provide not a hero (as the hard-hearted Giuliani ironically became), but a forceful, compelling new discourse about what this storm destroyed, why it cannot be permitted to facilitate the Americanization of a black city, who is owed what, and who must pay. All cities would benefit from that voice. It's not that New Orleans mayor Ray Nagin is a bad mayor per se. History may well reward his caution during much of the months-long cleanup interregnum (though it won't forget his inane ruminations on Martin Luther King Day about New Orleans being a "chocolate city" again after earning God's wrath).[23] It's that he has yet to marshal a limbo-defeating vision, become known to his constituents for his love under pressure, pledge his undying support for the most vulnerable among them, challenge insurance companies or expose capitalist carpetbagging. While lecturing black people about failing to help each other, he has made no provision for tens of thousands of poor black New Orleanians. Nor has he once openly antagonized business interests, which is necessary in such a crisis and not fatal to the markets disasters create; some qualified antagonism shows that the public sphere is aware of the tensions among the interests involved and knows that the interests are not equal. Healthy antagonism shows a skepticism for the processes Hirsch described when he warned of Americanization. And finally, clear and forceful black leadership would undermine New Orleans's long reputation as a juvenile delinquent child-city of a corrupt state, a Big Easy of impulsivity, profligacy, and adolescent ethics. Now, more than ever, this history reflects on current leadership, just as urban decline nationally is often blamed on the failures of black elected officials who inherited cities abandoned by whites. In this sense I rescind the village analogy. What New Orleans faces is an urban crisis—not only a natural disaster—as challenging as any American city has ever faced.

REMEDIES AND RETURN

The blunderous rescue and recovery efforts undertaken by federal, state, and local agencies in the first two weeks after Katrina struck (and, to a lesser extent, Rita) was enough to move visibly exasperated journalists to tears and severely impacted President Bush's approval ratings. These two facts revealed rare mainstream acknowledgment of a breach of the social contract, particularly when it came to both race and class. Katrina's destruction exposed the devastating limbo of intense poverty and made it relevant. Public reaction was a momentary repudiation of negligence toward the poor, even a brief horror at one's own hatreds. As for the poor themselves, it has never been clear that people who live racially segregated, economically disconnected lives are consciously aware of how much they're despised by the mainstream.

Many know, but for most the knowledge may operate unconsciously, especially in nihilistic behaviors. It is rarely thought
about. Yet an amazing thing about the Katrina "rescue" was the
sense of recognition on the survivors' faces, as if to say, "They must
really hate me to leave me here so long." (That is another cruelty of
sudden death, the creeping realization of being left forever.) These
complementary awarenesses—"We must be hated, Lord!" and
"My God, we must have hated!"—the union of revelations concerning the humanist assumptions beneath our social contract, offered a historic moment of opportunity.

Predictably, it passed. The memory will be "raced." Soon this
history will become black, not American. And the problems, like
mourners at all those funerals, will belong to one color again.

Months after the rescue was complete, the long-awaited plans
of the mayor's Bring New Orleans Back Committee contained no
direct provisions for the displaced poor and renters. Their well-
publicized circumstances provoked no particular planning ur-
gency among the rebuilding planners. A hundred and fifty days
after Katrina turned into breeze, a former resident of New Orleans
public housing could learn no more about her future than from a
Web site explaining that the projects would remain closed for the
foreseeable future. Instead, the "plans" somehow expected poor
renters and owners mysteriously to organize their neighbors (even
though there's no central public data bank), develop a consensus,
and execute their own plan of neighborhood return, which, only if
it satisfies some arbitrary standard, will be matched by a governmental investment of resources and protection. If they fail to prove
their collective commitment to rebuild with sufficient investment,
their homes *may* be razed.[24] The government will know a neighborhood worth rebuilding when it sees one. To further ensure

paralysis, the Bush administration withdrew its support for a popular bill in Congress under which the government would have guaranteed both homeowners and banks a buyout.

This Reagan-style approach to the demonstrably vulnerable among us is not leadership (or, as it was so cynically labeled in the late 1980s and 1990s, "empowerment"), but more limbo for the despised and an even larger repudiation of the social contract. There isn't the slightest courage to acknowledge the needs of the city's now famous poor. It all but guarantees their exile.[25] Without their own city and state to protect them, they have become pinballs in a FEMA game of rotating hotel evictions. Survivors would simply discover notes under their hotel room doors that the federal government was ending housing vouchers in 90 days, no, 120 days, no, by March 1. Yet by mid-February, *thousands* of empty FEMA trailers had rotted in the Arkansas mud while FEMA announced that entire families, dropped by buses wherever they had been dropped, must finally make their own permanent plans and get out.[26] The indifference had turned willful, the limbo calculated.[27]

Against the tease of early compassion, this limbo-reinforcing policymaking teaches the deepening irrelevance of fragile communities across America. Katrina's disastrous effects on New Orleans were only the extreme consequence for a nation of urban fault lines. This was but one sudden death in a country of slowly dying communities whose occasional passing goes barely noted. Clearer now, the floating corpses and malnourished neighborhoods are also the present effects of past racial discrimination, which help to condition the physical environment and the economic identities of millions of black urban residents across the United States. Yes, their *identities* because—like a televised riot and a videotaped beating, an Ebonics controversy, a perp walk on the nightly news, an antigang ordinance, a welfare-reform bill, the universally asserted ignorance of the O.J. jurors, or a bullet-ridden brutality victim whose killers walk free—Katrina's survivors will irreversibly be known for this latest spectacle of defeat. And they damned well know it. Forgetting them in the rebuilding plan will keep the stigma, like their impoverished status, fresh in their lives for many years to come. Looking back at the funerals, suddenly we're not all there anymore.

There must be better revelations about what to do now. Of course Katrina represents a fatal collision of race and class, but there's no revelation in that discovery. The revelation comes with a commitment to taking the necessary steps to transform chronic constraints into active capacity. We have always known this but never done it. The details of New Orleans's reconstruction are more appropriately argued elsewhere, and there are undoubtedly many good ideas already at work. But when the focus is returned to the city's persistently poor, the core principles of reconstruction amount to a restoration of a neglected, often violated social contract. What victims of both the storm and the city's history need is plain: solid jobs (in a labor economy offering more than hawking T-shirts to tourists) and affordable housing (in a landscape characterized by shared benefits and burdens and secure against the threat of inundation). Both may be accomplished through vehicles of conditional public finance and regulatory presumptions—in other words, a jobs trust idea and a land trust idea. Means-eligible residents must be favored under both ideas.

In a jobs trust, the first step is to condition any public subsidies for reconstruction work on high thresholds of local labor. New Orleans will be flush with housing and commercial construction–related employment for at least a decade, which is usually good work if you can find it. A firm would receive no public money for labor-intensive economic development projects unless it first demonstrated active efforts to secure workers who could show residency in the city for, say, three of the past five years. Local job applicants would enjoy a presumption or preference over others, especially if they came from particularly hard-hit areas of the city. This is as commonplace as the police department hiring rules in many cities and as radical as minority set-asides. However, the latter is unnecessary given the demographics of New Orleans's displaced population. Of course, the mere offering of jobs is not enough; people need support services as well, such as skills-training workshops and apprenticeship programs, temporary housing, child care, and related services aimed at facilitating the productive return of a traumatized workforce. Some of the federal pledge of *$62 billion* in Katrina assistance can be earmarked for these ends. So huge a public investment creates its own lasting market realities. This cannot be merely a supply-side hope, therefore, but a government-driven commitment binding employers. Expensive? Probably, but New Orleans's poverty was never cheap.

However, the jobs trust notion relies on a land trust notion. The presumption that would condition public spending for residential land use projects is that both renters and homeowners who wish to return to New Orleans should be given every reasonable chance. A reasonable chance may not include return to an exact location whose safety from the next storm cannot or should not be assured within several years, but it would be based on clear criteria. Key among those would be that every government-backed expenditure for housing development must satisfy the requirement that a proposed usage has no segregative effect; that it contributes to a fair distribution of income groups among residents; and that it can be integrated into an environmentally sound plan for public infra-structure, access to health care, schools, and employment centers. New Urbanist ideas for more integrated community designs are al-ready being considered for other areas of the Gulf Coast, but this one would explicitly provide for expanded affordability aimed at meeting the needs of New Orleans's displaced poor.[28] Like inclu-sionary zoning, it will inevitably—but not exclusively—rely on in-centives to market actors, such as developers, to achieve new housing goals. Like the historic districts that abound in older cities, a land trust may be quite technical in preserving specific land uses for certain socially desirable ends, or it may be encom-passed within the legal requirements of a master plan. Yet, unlike what the city has offered returning residents, the land trust would constitute a virtual guarantee of government support for citizen return. It should be difficult for poor citizens of New Orleans *not* to find a home again, not the opposite.

But the reality of sudden death and the poverty of disaster is that, for any thousands already gone, there is no imminent return from limbo. There is only diaspora. For them, the opportunities for remaking our social contract will not be reflected in land and jobs trusts in New Orleans, but in the supports we extend to dis-placed families and individuals in Houston, Atlanta, Los Angeles, and Newark. In most cases, their chaotic lives in new and unfamil-iar places will contend with the old and familiar constraints that face poor people across American cities—only more of them. Low wages for part-time work with no benefits—yet higher costs of liv-ing than in New Orleans. The need for affordable day care, driver's licenses, and counseling—but disconnected from informal sup-port networks and public agencies that know their histories. Ka-trina made them the poor *plus*. That extra degree of hardship is the effect of diaspora. It ought to be the measure of our policies. Because if programs can help effectively rebuild these lives, whole neighborhoods may follow.

The governmental amnesia for New Orleans's once-pitiable poor is not an accidental illness. First on the agenda of any American city, according to conventional urban planning, is to jettison households who use more public services than they pay for in taxes. That this belief is so widely held—an understanding that the interests of the middle class are incompatible with those of the poor—is a testament to Americanization. It puts the lie to a social contract ideal.

Yet just because it's been said and said again doesn't make it true. New Orleans could be the model of a major city that once again demonstrated its difference. The markets for land and employment are wide open in many parts of the city, waiting to be remade by public funding and local and regional planning. In the next several years, sound and inclusionary policies could bring the convergence of interests—white/black, middle-/working-class—rarely tried in this country and herald a new ideal of citizenship. Whether or not the specific principles of land and job trusts proposed here are followed in the cities that are watching is less important than embracing the rationales behind them. The punishing binaries of Americanization are poised to be frustrated and shattered; New Orleans cannot wait for their accidental breakup. The dignitary rights of a thousand corpses deserve this effort. The struggles of many thousands gone warrant the right to return. It was love that brought us to those funerals after all, not shame. Bury this limbo.

NOTES

1. Arnold R. Hirsch, "Simply a Matter of Black and White: The Transformation of Race and Politics in Twentieth-Century New Orleans," in *Creole New Orleans: Race and Americanization* ed. Arnold R. Hirsch and Logsdon (1992), 265.

2. William Julius Williams, *The Truly Disadvantaged* (Baton Rouge: Louisiana State University Press, 1996), 12–50.

3. Ibid.

4. The Brookings Institution Metropolitan Policy Program, *New Orleans After the Storm: Lessons from the Past, a Plan for the Future,* October 2005, 8. Unemployment statistics count only workers who have actively sought employment within a twenty-six-week period. Those who have been out of work for longer than that are deemed "nonparticipants" or out of the labor force, and their numbers are not reflected in unemployment rates.

5. See, e.g., Alfred W. Blumrosen and Ruth G. Blumrosen, *The Reality of Intentional Job Discrimination in Metropolitan America: Louisiana,* available at http://www.EEO1.com. In a study of 1999 employment data supplied by 1,226 Louisiana employers to the federal government, the authors found that in the New Orleans standard metropolitan statistical area, blacks faced discrimination in the following industries at the following rates: hospitals (60 percent), grocery stores (60 percent), ship/boat building/repairing (61.54 percent), and commercial banks (76.92 percent).

6. Martha Mahoney, "Law and Racial Geography: Public Housing and the Economy in New Orleans," *Stanford Law Review* 42 (1990): 1251; 1254.

7. Ibid, 1276.

8. Ibid.

9. Brookings Institution, *New Orleans After the Storm,* 24–25.

10. Bill Lambrecht, "U.S. Gov't Ignored Advice After Flood of '93," *St. Louis Post-Dispatch,* September 13, 2005

11. Brookings Institution, *New Orleans After the Storm,* 15–17.

12. Ibid.

13. Ibid.

14. Ibid., 19.

15. Brookings Institution, "Key Indicators of Entrenched Poverty," Brookings Metropolitan Policy Program 2005, using U.S. Census and U.S. Department of Housing and Urban Development data.

16. Brookings Institution, *New Orleans After the Storm,* 5, 17.

17. Ibid., 11.

18. Ibid., 9–10.

19. Ibid., 10–11.

20. Brookings Institution, "Key Indicators."

21. Comparisons based on data contained in charts, Brookings Institution, *New Orleans After the Storm,* 6–8.

22. I may have been lucky. See Jordan Flaherty and Jennifer Vitry, "(More) Loss and Displacement in New Orleans," www.alternet.org/story/30707/, posted January 12, 2006. The authors report that despite the officially ordered evacuation by all residents, many people found that their homes had been burglarized. By threat of armed National Guard, residents are not allowed to return, yet many have lost valuables since Katrina. It should be noted that B.W. Cooper may be the largest tenant-managed housing development in the United States. Ibid.

23. See Brett Martel, "Storms Payback from God, Nagin Says; Mayor Faults War, Blacks' Infighting," *Washington Post,* January 7, 2006. Specifically, Nagin said the following: "It's time for us to come together. It's time for us to rebuild New Orleans—the one that should be a chocolate New Orleans. . . . This city will be a majority African American city. It's the way God wants it to be. You can't have New Orleans no other way. It wouldn't be New Orleans."

24. See Urban Planning Committee Report, www.cityofno.com, www.bringneworleansback.org (last visited January 25, 2006).

25. James Dao, "Study Says 80% of New Orleans Blacks May Not Return," *New York Times*, January 27, 2006. The Logan study also found that as many as half the city's white population might not return.

26. See Eric Lipton, "Trailer Dispute May Mean Thousands Will Go Unused," *New York Times*, February 14, 2006.

27. A few months later, FEMA would jerk the chain again, this time arbitrarily withdrawing eligibility for 12-month vouchers to approximately 55,000 families displaced by Katrina. See Shaila Dewan, "Evacuees Find Housing Grants Will End Soon," *New York Times*, April 27, 2006.

28. See Neal Pierce, " 'Charrette' Offers Hope to Bring Back New Orleans," *Houston Chronicle*, January 30, 2006.

2.

KATRINA: THE AMERICAN DILEMMA REDUX*
Sheryll Cashin

*Poverty has roots in a history of racial discrimination, which cut off
generations from the opportunity of America. . . . We have a duty to
confront this poverty with bold action. . . . Let us rise above the
legacy of inequality.*
—George Bush, Jackson Square, New Orleans, September 15, 2005

*Five days in this motherf—ing attic
I can't use the cellphone I keep getting static
Dying 'cause they lying instead of telling us the truth . . .
Screwed 'cause they say they're coming back for us, too
but that was three days ago and I don't see no rescue . . .
Swam to the store, tryin' to look for food
Corner store's kinda flooded so I broke my way through
Got what I could but before I got through
News say the police shot a black man trying to loot.*
—Excerpt from "George Bush Don't Like Black People" (remixed
by the Legendary K.O, words by Big Mon and Damien)

The stark disconnect between President George Bush's professed,
unfulfilled intent to attack the racial dimensions of poverty and

inequality in our nation and the hip-hop generation's brilliant send-up of Kanye West's discomfiting cry, "George Bush doesn't care about black people," mirrors the social gulf that is American race relations. Most whites were of the view that the gut-wrenching delays in FEMA's response had nothing to do with race. Most black people, on the other hand, felt in their bones that this delay would not have happened if the majority of people stranded at the Superdome and New Orleans Convention Center had been white.[1] West inaptly articulated a powerful frustration and anger among many black folks. Of course there was no way to test the veracity of our collective intuition. But I did witness hints of it. A local National Public Radio affiliate in my hometown of Washington, D.C., featured an interview with a D.C.-area woman who, by voice and response to events, I took to be white. She had been stranded at the Ritz Carlton in New Orleans, which is four minutes by car from the convention center. Days before buses began to arrive at the Superdome and convention center, she described a veritable SWAT team that commandeered more buses than were actually needed to escort all of the guests in her hotel safely out of the city.[2] This minor anecdote proves nothing, of course. But it and other stories stick with me: for example, the revelation that the White House had been alerted forty-eight hours before Katrina hit about the storm's likely impact; a detailed analysis eerily predicted much of what ultimately happened in New Orleans, including the breach of the levees and catastrophic loss of life and property. The inept response of the federal government surely reflects incompetence rather than overt racism. But many African Americans, myself included, couldn't help but feel that the risks to a then–70 percent black, heavily poor city were devalued.

There is much to reflect on in contemplating the one-year anniversary of the Katrina disaster. Since that painful Labor Day weekend, I have been fixated mostly on what the hurricane and its aftermath indicate about the state of race relations, and the geographic dimensions of the problem. At the dawn of the twentieth century W.E.B. DuBois famously wrote that *the* American problem in the 1900s would be "the problem of the color line." A century and a few years later, Katrina showed that a color line of a certain type continues to haunt us. In our collective, ugly Superdome moment the America that is normally invisible to the masses was thrust into view. The ghetto was moved by natural disaster, and man-made ineptitude, from low-lying, out-of-the-way areas to the public square of cable television. The ghetto is the holdover issue in America's three-hundred-year struggle with race.

The people literally and figuratively left behind put a face on concentrated black poverty for a nation that has long since moved on to other business. Outside of a ghetto context, one could argue that American race relations are much improved. The same America that shuns the black ghetto has made Oprah one of the richest women on the planet. The diplomatic face of American foreign policy is now that of a black woman, who succeeded a black man. No other predominantly white country in the world can match such examples of stratospheric success of a historically oppressed racial minority. It is not uncommon for the number one movies at the box office to be vehicles for black actors. It no longer takes having the chiseled good looks of Will Smith or the classic beauty of Halle Berry to have mass crossover appeal. Samuel L. Jackson, in all his wonderful blackness, is also getting paid.

Surely there is something to the shibboleth of America as the land of opportunity—a place where a person truly can be judged solely by the content of her character. The civil rights movement resulted in more than just psychic benefits. In 1950 the black poverty rate was 72 percent; a large majority of "my people" lived below the poverty line, and for many, middle-class status or a decent-paying job was an elusive dream.[3]

But then there are the depressing statistics. Today 24 percent of black folks still live in poverty—about double the national average. If I were a young black male I would rather have come of age in the late seventies than today. Why? Because today there are more black men behind bars than there are in college, a sharp reversal since 1980, when black men enrolled in higher education outnumbered black men behind bars by three to one. The effects of an unforgiving penal system are harshest in the ghettos, where a majority of black men can be under some form of criminal supervision.

This leads me to my chief observation about the way America relates to black people. While nonblacks can be fascinated appropriators of black culture, the primary or primal response to blackness when it is experienced en masse seems to be fear. We do pretty well in individual encounters or from the safe distance of the big or small screen in experiencing blackness in a neutral, or maybe even a positive, way. America can relate to, even celebrate black individuals. The broad appeal of a Barack Obama suggests that the vast majority of Americans do not harbor a conscious race prejudice. Still, if social surveys are to be believed, the group that all nonblacks have the most antipathy toward sharing their life space with is black people. In psychological tests designed to measure ingrained, rapid responses rather than considered, rational ones, a black face engenders a negative response, even when the person responding is also black.[4]

After several years researching the state of race and class integration, or the lack thereof, in the United States, I came to the conclusion that concentrated black poverty—the black ghetto—is at the center of racial tensions in this country. The black poor are the only demographic group in America singled out for a degree of segregation that demographers call hypersegregation—extremely isolated neighborhoods where more than 40 percent of residents live below the poverty line. The technical meaning of this term is less important than the fact that no other group—not poor whites, Latinos, Asians, or even Native Americans—experiences this degree of isolation from the American mainstream.

Residents of hypersegregated ghetto neighborhoods constitute just 1 percent of the national population but the ghetto looms large in how black folks are perceived. The ghetto is an alternative universe: one where the standard language is "Ebonics," where more adult males can be unemployed than working, and where the prison system plays a more dominant role in the lives of young men than the education system. Even before hardened criminals took to the streets of New Orleans in Katrina's wake, the signatures and behaviors of the ghetto were familiar to many Americans. The swagger of "thug life," exaggerated for consumers of hip-hop culture, is more than just performance art. The violence and death that can permeate high-poverty black neighborhoods are real. So-called ghetto behaviors rationalize fear and stereotyping of black people, as the black mayor of Baton Rouge demonstrated last fall when he lectured devastated evacuees about not descending into lawlessness.[5] Suddenly all blacks from the Big Easy were equated with the worst criminals.

When Katrina first hit, I had the surreal experience of observing her impact from the "neutral" territory of Montreal, Canada. A Labor Day weekend vacation quickly turned dim as my husband and I watched helplessly from a hotel room while the crisis intensified. Over and over again we were treated to the contrast of Canadian and U.S. media coverage. The Canadian, French, and British outlets that were available to us did not mindlessly rerun footage of "looters" that was stock fare on CNN, FOX, and other U.S. outlets. It was too easy for U.S. media outlets to play to stereotype. Many of the reports of shooting and looting in New Orleans turned out not to be accurate.[6]

The same stereotypical associations that led media producers to portray people of color as looters, and white people who took what they needed as survivors, play out daily in American life. For example, in a recent study of employer hiring practices published in the *Wall Street Journal*, black males with *no* criminal record did worse than white males who *did* have a record. Low-income African Americans especially struggle against the weighted assumptions projected onto them by everyone else, including their higher-income brethren. Yet studies also show that when ghetto residents are given the opportunity to live in middle-class neighborhoods, as are most poor whites in this country, they improve significantly in education and employment. Ghetto behaviors are intrinsic to high-poverty places, not people.

Despite the clear progress we have made since the civil rights revolution, in expanding economic opportunity and the ranks of the black middle class, the number of neighborhoods marked by ghetto poverty has increased steadily. Concentrated black poverty was created by intentional public policy choices, including urban renewal, ill-conceived public housing, and highways intentionally laid to cut blacks off from the "good" side of town. Different policy choices could replace ghettos with vibrant mixed-income neighborhoods.

The potential silver lining in the Katrina disaster was that, in having to start from scratch in so many neighborhoods, we had the opportunity to do things differently. The international shame of images worthy of a third world nation, or impertinent assertions of racial indifference from the likes of a Kanye West, may have led President Bush to make an eloquent pledge to tackle directly the underlying issues of racially identifiable poverty. But in the ensuing weeks it became evident that politics as usual had returned to Washington, D.C. Stories of misspent FEMA funds, of Small Business Administration–backed low-interest loans flowing to wealthy neighborhoods but not to low-income ones, and of a New Orleans recovery plan that discouraged rather than encouraged low-income people of color to return suggested that rebuilding would reflect the nearly universal pattern of race and class segregation that typifies the American landscape.[7]

My hope had been that we would seriously rethink past mistakes by giving poor evacuees housing vouchers and placement assistance that provided them with a meaningful shot at living in middle-class settings. Rather than utilize Housing and Urban Development's existing section 8 housing voucher program to pursue just such a strategy, the Bush administration offered confusing, short-term, FEMA-administered housing assistance, even as it was proposing to gut the very programs that were most likely to have the bold impact Bush promised in his Jackson Square speech.[8] In addition to providing housing vouchers to those trapped in high-poverty ghetto neighborhoods, a saner housing strategy for the nation would redevelop formerly high-poverty neighborhoods in ways that ensure that middle-class people, and hence middle-class norms, predominate. At the same time, the low-income housing stock would need to be replaced and dispersed. And we could offer federal incentives that encourage *all* communities to develop affordable housing.

Over time, such policies would ensure that no neighborhood is overwhelmed by poverty. They would also enable the privileged to live in an ever more diverse society without fear. In my view, Katrina and her aftermath demonstrate how our race relations have been shaped by the physical organization of the American metropolis and how our physical organization has shaped our race relations. In a sense, we are stuck. Fear of blacks in numbers led to the adoption of public policies that created the black ghetto (and also created privileged white space heavily buffered from concentrated black poverty). The nonmainstream behaviors and norms incubated in the ghetto, in turn, rationalize fear on the part of mainstream America of poor blacks, which in turn makes it very difficult to adopt saner public policies that enable poor black people to live in middle-class settings. The Katrina debacle offered a rare moment for potential empathy with the plight of the black poor—but the media's heavy play to stereotype about the ghetto mirrored Americans' worst fears, exposing, again, the conundrum we face as a nation in transcending our tortured race relations.

NOTES

* Unless otherwise noted, the empirical claims in this chapter are supported in Professor Cashin's book, *The Failures of Integration: How Race and Class Are Undermining the American Dream* (New York: PublicAffairs, 2004).

1. See Susan Page and Maria Puente, "Polls Show Racial Divide on Storm Response," *USA Today,* September 12, 2005, www.usatoday.com/news/nation/2005-09-12-katrina-poll_x.htm, last visited February 2, 2006.

2. The author heard this interview on WAMU, 88.5 FM, in Washington, D.C., the week of September 5, 2005, but it is not available on the station's Web site.

3. Michael B. Katz and Mark J. Stern, "Poverty in Twentieth-Century America," American at the Millennium Project, Working Paper no. 7 (November 2001), 34 table 3, www.sp2.upenn.edu/america2000/wp7all.pdf, last visited February 2, 2006.

4. See, e.g., Jerry Kang, "Trojan Horses of Race," *Harvard Law Review* 118 (2005), 1490.

5. Melvin Holden, Mayor of Baton Rouge, Chaos and Catastrophe in New Orleans; FEMA Briefing (September 1, 2005), http://transcripts.cnn.com/TRANSCRIPTS/0509/01/lt.03.html.

6. See Donna Britt, "In Katrina's Wake, Inaccurate Rumors Sullied Victims," *Washington Post,* September 30, 2005.

7. See Leslie Eaton, "Louisiana Tries to Show It Is Handling Its Relief Money Honestly," *New York Times,* October 20, 2005; James Dao, "Study Say 80% of New Orleans Blacks May Not Return," *New York Times,* January 27, 2006; Adam Nossiter, "Fight Grows in New Orleans on Demolition and Rebuilding," *New York Times,* January 5, 2006; Leslie Eaton and Ron Nixon, "Loans to Homeowners Along Gulf Coast Lag," *New York Times,* December 15, 2005.

8. See, e.g., Spencer S. Hsu and Ceci Connolly, "Housing the Displaced Is Rife with Delays," *Washington Post,* September 23, 2005; Jason Deparle, "Lack of Section 8 Vouchers for Storm Evacuees Highlights Rift over Housing Program," *New York Times,* November 24, 2005; Editorial, "The Katrina Housing Debacle," *New York Times,* November 24, 2005.

Part Two

CLASS, POLITICS, AND THE POLITICS OF RACE

3

THE PERSISTENCE OF RACE POLITICS AND THE RESTRAINT OF RECOVERY IN KATRINA'S WAKE
John Valery White

"I want to make sure that some of these thugs and looters that are out shooting officers in New Orleans don't come here and do the same. I am not going to allow a New Orleans situation, shooting at people and looting, to happen here in Baton Rouge," said Baton Rouge's mayor, Melvin "Kip" Holden, igniting a maelstrom of hysterical rumor that would, along with rumors of mayhem in New Orleans, mark the beginning of the end of efforts to rebuild New Orleans. Holden's statement was surprising and disappointing, coming from a black mayor whose election was viewed as a victory for black and progressive voters in the state. But it expressed the long-standing stigmatization of black New Orleanians that has operated since the storm to severely restrict rebuilding efforts. It also foreshadowed a post-Katrina racial politics aimed at dispersing black voters, remaking New Orleans, and securing a new political order.

Mayor Holden's "thugs" statement created hysteria in Baton Rouge and hampered rescue efforts on Wednesday, August 31, as evacuation efforts were just beginning, as thousands stood stranded in their New Orleans homes, and as increasing numbers were gathering at the Superdome and the convention center. As the crisis escalated, Holden's office announced that Baton Rouge needed to "get out of the shelter business."[1] Then emerged baseless reports of robberies and muggings. Talk radio spread stories of rapes in the streets; SWAT teams were called to the city's River Center convention facility, where five thousand evacuees were being housed; city offices were closed; and evacuees from St. Bernard Parish were turned away.[2] Louisiana State University chancellor Shawn O'Keefe advised students and faculty to lock down buildings and go home on "confirmed reports of civil unrest in Baton Rouge." Rumors eventually prompted the state to close offices in the capital city, where rescue efforts were headquartered.[3]

Four months after the storm, rebuilding efforts had stalled as a consensus emerged that the city should not be rebuilt to accommodate most of its residents. Underlying this consensus is a desire to change the city's demographics, a desire itself rooted in the racial politics that compelled Holden's statement. The antirebuilding consensus has created an atmosphere of distrust as residents and observes recognize that all rebuilding proposals represent choices over who *should* return. Residents know they are to be displaced, as no affordable housing is discussed, though two-thirds of displaced residents were renters. This is a context where the "third world" images of desperate people huddled in front of the convention center, hungry, thirsty, and forgotten, have become grounds for fear and derision, not empathy. The symbolic force of the catastrophe has been transformed by the peculiar racial politics, permitting Americans and Louisianians alike to reject responsibility for the concentration of racialized poverty on display.

Despite angry rebuttals, race became a major way to understand the crisis. Many argued powerfully and simply that the slow governmental response would not have been tolerated had disaster struck (white) New England. The lack of momentum on the rebuilding, periodic statements rejecting rebuilding altogether (from House Speaker Dennis Hastert even), and descriptions of the future city as smaller, less poor, and less black vest the argument that race played a role in the crisis with tremendous symbolic power. However, this symbolic framing of the crisis saps any discussion of the depth and realism necessary for serious analysis of the problem of race and poverty. It also obscures the real political limitations that restrict the recovery effort and which work to prevent the return of the city's black residents.

Set in symbolic terms, the discussion of race and Katrina takes on the same tone as arguments that Louisiana built inadequate levees (it did not, as the Army Corps of Engineers designed and built the levees) or that the levees were dynamited (true during the Great Flood of 1929, but unsupported today). That is, discussion of the images of desperate evacuees—most poor, most black, all haggard—becomes an unbounded riff on the imagery, an interpretative exercise. The symbolic rendering of Katrina's racial dimension is in accord with a discussion of race and poverty that utilize snapshots of poor neighborhoods to isolate an "underclass" responsible for its own situation. Such a view of the city and the catastrophe permit the kind of wishful thinking that seems to follow every event that reveals America's shameful racial inequality. As with the Rodney King riots in 1991, commentators talked about how, this time, perhaps, America would begin to confront its racial-inequality issues. But as the shame passes, the momentum for change rapidly evaporates, replaced only by conspiracy theories that promise to explain why nothing changed. The abstraction itself invites psychobabble-laden analyses of the American condition, all the while ignoring extant political conditions. Ultimately, this type of lazy analysis invites ridiculous neo-Maoist arguments (maybe, if things got worse, people would rise up), underlies calls for Tupac Amaru–like terrorism from coffee-shop philosophers, and animates nostalgic protest marches, while ignoring the political context of these crises.

Ironically, Mayor Holden's statement illuminates the role race (that is, race politics) plays in the post-Katrina story. It duplicates the national response to rumors of mayhem during the evacuation of New Orleans: both were unsupported but, once spoken, triggered a veritable orgy of speculation that relieved outsiders of responsibility for the catastrophe. Holden's statement was more insidious because he is the black mayor of the state capital and spoke of black New Orleanians. Mayor Holden permitted *Louisianians,* who had before then put race, class, and geography aside to rescue their fellows, to begin repudiating the black New Orleans of their fears. His statement, more than the rumors of mayhem, initiated a process of rejecting the conditions necessary to effectively rebuild the city. The political limitations that underlay Holden's statement structure and constrain the rebuilding effort, limiting the prospects for the city.

This Essay argues that real racial politics have doomed the rebuilding effort. First, it highlights how the need to repopulate the city has been hampered by the desire to keep most of its poor black residents from returning. Second, it sets out why and how the desire to change the city's demographics have become the key aspect of rebuilding planning. The Essay argues that state electoral politics prevents officials from developing temporary villages in the region, though necessary to the return of New Orleans's citizens and for the successful rebuilding of the city and the state's economy.

The discussion that follows examines the rare opportunity for partisan advantage that animates the Administration's weak support for redevelopment. Finally, I detail the political limitations of the key black actors, Mayors Holden and Nagin. Though their performance might have cast doubt on black politics, it rather shows the insidiousness of race politics. It becomes clear that, apart from interpretation of the symbols of the catastrophe, the racially charged political context in which Katrina occurred was quite sufficient to forestall rebuilding of one of America's great cities.

REBUILDING A CITY WITHOUT PEOPLE

The scope of the catastrophe in New Orleans is on a par with the devastating earthquakes that have obliterated cities around the world, like Bam, Iran, or with the tsunami of December 2004. Though the death toll was (fortunately) relatively low, the devastation dwarfs recent American tragedies. Winds damaged a large number of buildings; the storm surge destroyed whole towns along the Mississippi and Louisiana coasts and flooded New Orleans East; and levee breaches flooded most of the rest of the city. The bulk of the city's housing stock is destroyed, rendering large swaths of the city uninhabitable. Many residents lost everything.

Despite the scope of the devastation, too many commentators mistakenly believe that the catastrophe can be remedied, as with previous hurricanes, with several years of enterprising effort by individual landowners. But New Orleans is a city imperiled because too many of its residents are gone. The storm emptied the city of 500,000 and left the suburbs without a vital center. The metropolitan area's 1.3 million population has been roughly halved, and for almost a month, most residents of the metropolitan area were barred from their homes and businesses. Four months after the storm, more than 250,000 people continued to live in other states, and nearly as many were displaced within Louisiana and Mississippi. Many of the 100,000 people who had returned to New Orleans lived in hotels at the beginning of 2006.

The return of New Orleans's citizens is its key development need. But repopulation of the city is the need most frustrated by the politics of the pre- and post-Katrina worlds. Those who speak of rebuilding acknowledge that citizens are required to breathe life into the city, to support economic activity, and to provide labor and consumers for businesses. However, those same people speak ominously about a "new" city, with a "different" population, with good (public) schools, without crime, and (often) without poverty. Despite the desperate need for citizens, there is a glee with which some speak of taking advantage of the storm to rid the city of its poor.

The paradox is that New Orleans is addicted to low-wage workers. In 2003 Louisiana was second in both the percentage of workers earning minimum wage (5.2 percent) and percentage of workers earning less than $7.15 per hour (25.5 percent).[4] ACORN's Living Wage Resource Center estimated in 2001 that forty-seven thousand workers in New Orleans (10 percent of the population) earned less than the $6.15 minimum wage that ACORN had proposed the city adopt. As their study also showed, most of these minimum wage jobs are concentrated in the hotels and restaurants that were central to the city's multibillion-dollar pre-Katrina tourism industry.[5] For that industry and the city, getting low-wage workers back to work is crucial. The inevitable wage pressure in the depopulated city has prompted complaints in the service sector about mythical $6,000 "signing bonuses" at fast-food restaurants and $8-an-hour cleanup and construction jobs. A food-processing company in Houma, Louisiana and a suburban New Orleans restaurateur spoke shamelessly on National Public Radio of needing to recruit workers from Mexico "willing to work" at the minimum wage they were offering.[6]

The city's employment crisis is obscured by the widespread belief that black workers are unwilling to work. Invoking the "black underclass" trope, commentators have seized on the images of the Superdome and convention center to argue that New Orleans's black residents were a huge underclass of unwilling workers. New Orleans was a troubled city with high crime rates and poor public schools, but the image of a massive underclass is an inaccurate portrait of pre-Katrina New Orleans. According to the nonprofit Initiative for a Competitive Inner City, more than 87 percent of the city's "inner-city" residents were employed. The organization, which defines "inner cities" as "urban areas that are economically distressed," found that "New Orleans' economy had an inordinate reliance on its working poor." Contrary to the easy "underclass" dismissals of the city's poor population, "the majority of its residents had jobs but remained impoverished."[7] Moreover, the popular conception of black workers as less attractive than immigrant workers, especially from Latin America, is awkward in New Orleans, a city with a long tradition of immigration from Latin America and where as many as 150,000 people (more than 10 percent of the city's pre-Katrina metropolitan population) were Honduran American (many of whom were black).[8]

Before Katrina, New Orleans did little for its working poor. State courts had declared a voter-adopted minimum-wage increase unconstitutional, the city's schools were ignored (except when invoked to advance the voucher movement), and the city's housing projects sat in ruin (except when razed for lucrative development projects). When Katrina hit, the accumulated prejudices against the city's working poor were unleashed in a barely contained expression of joy at the possibility that the working poor would leave and never return. The city's new paradox—how to get the low-wage workers on which it depended without the poverty to which their low wages consigned them—has been ignored. In the short term the rebuilding effort, managed largely by Houston-based recipients of FEMA contracts, has relied on transient labor from around the country as well as from Mexico and Central America. These workers' lack of accompanying families has permitted them to live in austere quarters, most often located and provided by their employers. In the long term, this is not an effective solution to the city's needs. Nevertheless, racial politics have conspired to point the city, state, and federal government definitively in the direction of dissuading most of the city's black working poor from returning.

LOCAL POLITICS, OR HOW TO DISPERSE BLACK VOTERS

Mayor Holden's statement reflects a statewide demonization of black New Orleanians that colors otherwise vague statements like a "new start," a "better city," and a city "without the old problems." These statements are fairly read as optimism that a city without poverty can be created from the wreck of the flood. Everyone wants to preserve the culture that underlies the food, the street musicians and second-liners, the jazz, but no one wants the working poor who lived these "quaint," touristic lives. Everyone wants to improve the city's institutions, but not for the city's poor pre-Katrina residents.

These contradictions are ignored because the post-Katrina debate is polluted by implicit questioning of the legitimacy of black politics. New Orleans has been in decline for many years. The city was in the 1950s the largest and most economically vital city in the South, headquarters of several Fortune 500 shipping, mining, and oil-exploration companies. Two decades later New Orleans had been eclipsed by several other southern cities that raided it for its companies and industries. When Katrina struck, the executive employees of the only two Fortune 500 companies to claim the city as home, Entergy and Freeport-McMoRan, were mostly based in other cities. Nationally, the demise of New Orleans has been explained by the state's corruption and by the very closed society of New Orleans elites that made it a hard place to do business, exacerbated by poor schools, the lack of space to grow, and a large poor population. But among Louisiana's elites, New Orleans's demise is blamed on the takeover of the city by black politicians in the late 1970s and 1980s. The post-Katrina dreams of a "new" New Orleans are thus part delusion—denial by New Orleans elites of their own role in the city's demise—and part excitement—destruction of the political order they blame for the city's decline.

New Orleans's political transformation is an intensification of the story of southern urban politics. More than other southern cities, New Orleans was an electoral juggernaut. High voter-registration levels (268,513 of roughly 480,000 in 2002) and turnout (usually the highest in the South), significant numbers of black and progressive residents, and a large population in proportion to the state produced powerful voting blocs for candidates that won the city's favor. Thus, the same New Orleans that lost the NFL's Pro Bowl in 1967 because its hotels would not house black players elected its first black mayor less than ten years later and proceeded to play a crucial role in all statewide contests thereafter.

This rapid shift destabilized urban power relationships and accelerated white flight to the suburbs. It also led many to regard the city's politics as inherently suspect, a tradition disturbingly reminiscent of Reconstruction-era dismissals of black political agency mocked in early Mardi Gras parades.

The complicated story of local political change drives the desire to "revitalize" New Orleans by excluding a large proportion of its black residents. This desire, however, directly contradicts the city's addiction to minimum-wage labor. The city's only remaining major industry, tourism, relies upon the low-wage labor of these residents. Moreover, New Orleanians' uncommon attachment to their city will likely require the kind of total effort at exclusion that will overexclude. New Orleans cast a spell on its residents that the devastation of Katrina alone is unlikely to break. Many poor New Orleanians had *never* left the city. Though living in one of the world's most traveled-to cities, other New Orleanians saw no reason to travel themselves. And those who have migrated to other cities struggled with the decision and now speak bitterly of the economic stagnation that forced their move. Any commitment to changing the city's demographics must actually prevent the return of the city's working poor despite the needs of the tourism industry. The plan to rebuild housing and neighborhoods unveiled in January does so.

If the desire to shape the city's future population is rooted in racial politics, it is also limited by it. Racial politics explains why Mayor Nagin's Bring New Orleans Back Committee did not solicit proposals from developers, urban planners, or architects, which would have sparked a public discussion of a future city, an urban plan, and housing stock that could facilitate the city's repopulation. One could imagine plans for internal levees and elevated multistory apartment and co-op housing that could accomodate the near-term return of much of the city's population *and* facilitate the future population growth necessary for the development of the city's economy beyond tourism. Instead, the committee worked in private, an approach crucial to achieving two goals rooted in racial politics: banning or restricting reconstruction in the most flooded areas, where the black working poor lived, while still allowing the possibility of redeveloping the upper-middle-class, overwhelmingly white Lake View neighborhood and the upper-middle-class black neighborhoods along Bayou St. Jean and in New Orleans East. Any plan that failed to permit the redevelopment of at least Lake View would be doomed; yet condemning poor neighborhoods alone would have exposed the plan's goal of excluding poor black residents.

Instead of a vigorous effort to include international expertise in the redevelopment of the city, perhaps helping to sustain outside interest in redeveloping the city and drawing essential private financing to the process, the city opted for a sustained period of silence. The lack of any indication of progress on developing a plan, or an open process including evacuees and outside interests, confirmed the image of the city as a closed place, hostile to business and corrupt. It also left evacuees with no indication of when and under what circumstances they might be able to begin rebuilding their lives. When the mayor's committee issued its rebuilding plan, four months after the disaster, much of the momentum for rebuilding the city had already been lost.

The closed process and limited ambition of the committee's plan for building housing reveal its goal of transforming the city's demographics. The plan for redevelopment is ingeniously constructed to shut down most of the areas where the city's black residents lived while not appearing to single out those neighborhoods. It holds out the prospect that some traditionally black neighborhoods will reemerge, but that hope is fleeting. The plan divides the city into a number of districts, the most flooded of which are subject to a rebuilding moratorium until at least May 2006. After that time neighbors who are able to show an intention to return can get the moratorium lifted. Upper-middle-class residents who own their property might meet this requirement, but it is very unlikely that renters in the neighborhoods of the working poor will.

Any success the committee's plan has at excluding the black working poor from the city's future will make it all but impossible to satisfy the city's labor needs during the crucial next several years. Nothing in the plan, which seems written in a universe bereft of multilevel, high-density housing, suggests that affordable housing will be constructed. Without accommodations for the city's low-wage workers (and better wages for them), the city's tourism-based economy cannot thrive, dooming the city before a "new" New Orleans can arise.

STATE POLITICS AND THE MISSING EVACUATION VILLAGES

The committee's plan assumes decentralized redevelopment accomplished by individual landowners in the areas permitted to rebuild. Whatever the wisdom of this lightly planned, market-based approach, it depends on the steady return of residents to the city. However, their return is limited by the resistance of the city, its neighboring communities, and the state to temporary housing developments for the displaced population. FEMA has proved slow to provide temporary housing, curiously announcing the acquisition of a large number of temporary trailers only after the big shelters in Louisiana and neighboring states had been emptied. However, when that announcement was made, only eight of Louisiana's sixty-four parishes were allowing trailers, thirty-two having barred trailer villages altogether. Even the New Orleans City Council has resisted the creation of temporary trailer villages within the city.[9] And, four months after the hurricane, the state had made no effort to require communities to permit trailer villages, despite a special hurricane-related legislative session. What FEMA trailers are in use are mostly in the driveways of homeowners intent on rebuilding, and mostly in the New Orleans suburbs.

Mayor Holden's worry about crime and disorder underlies the rejection of trailer villages, the consequences of which become clearer with even the most elementary understanding of Louisiana geography. The relatively steady curve of the coast from east to west abruptly drops at the Louisiana-Mississippi border. The extension of the curve of the coast through Louisiana, along Interstate 12 and then Interstate 10 from Baton Rouge westward, marks the rough division between swamp and dry ground. Until one crosses Lake Pontchartain or reaches Baton Rouge along the river, there is inadequate high ground for many temporary villages. Several trailer villages have been established in East Baton Rouge Parish (without the feared crime and disorder), but Baton Rouge is too far away for residents regularly working on rebuilding New Orleans. The natural place for sufficiently numerous temporary housing is on the "North Shore" of Lake Pontchartrain, in the very parishes that have been the recipients of "white flight" from New Orleans. That there are *no* trailer villages in those parishes testifies to the power of Mayor Holden's disorder message and to a deep, statewide commitment to a less black future New Orleans.

However, New Orleans cannot be rebuilt without a nearby place for workers and their families to live. The migrant workers from Mexico and elsewhere who have appeared, much to the consternation of the region's anti-immigrant types, cannot be expected to continue working if their families cannot join them. Currently, there is not adequate housing for them or for the New Orleans residents they replaced.

The contradiction for the North Shore parishes is that their economies depend on a viable New Orleans. Similarly, the state's economy—powered in its poor, rural parishes by state government spending—is imperiled by the loss of the 40 percent of state tax revenue produced in New Orleans. Reconstruction spending may temporarily offset some of the loss, but it is crucial for the state that New Orleans's economy bounce back. Revitalization of New Orleans simply requires substantial population growth on the North Shore. But such growth is unlikely, as the North Shore was the area of the state which, with Plaquemines Parish south of New Orleans, mounted Louisiana's most vicious resistance to the civil rights movement, produced the state's most vocal segregationists, and supported most strongly David Duke.

The failure of the state to require parishes to take on trailer villages is rooted in the peculiar race politics that haunt the catastrophe. Like the rest of the South, Louisiana has steadily been turning Republican. The basis for this shift is rooted in the overlapping moral and racial politics of the Republican Party. Although the party has been soft-pedaling race since taking over Congress, the Republican success in the South has been related to its becoming the "ethnic" party for white southerners. Southern Democrats have been elected (recently only in Louisiana) by relying on a solid black vote and by appealing to a rapidly shrinking pool of progressive and liberal white southerners. As liberal and progressive southerners have decreased in number and concentrated in cities, the Democratic Party in the South has lost ground, becoming a party of mostly black voters. In Louisiana, however, the large size of the black population (33 percent) has made it possible for moderate Democrats to reach out beyond progressive voters, appealing to local interests to build a sustainable coalition. This was the winning formula of Governor Kathleen Blanco (who was not supporter by the majority of black voters during the primaries) and of Senator Mary Landrieu (who was). Both defeated Republican opponents by capturing local issues (the dire effects of the Central American Free Trade Agreement on Louisiana's sugar industry, for example). Republicans such as Senator David Vitter and former governor Mike Foster have prevailed by successfully capturing local substantive issues and running on a combination of moral issues (Vitter's and Foster's reelection landslides) and race issues (Foster's first campaign).

The success of Louisiana Democrats such as Governor Blanco turns on their ability to appear focused on Louisiana issues while still being able to capture the black vote. With many of New Orleans's black voters displaced (and thus unreliable), Louisiana Democrats cannot afford to appear opposed to local interests even though doing so solidifies the dispersion of their (black) voting base. Thus, no state officials have challenged the not-in-my-backyard sentiments that have excluded trailer villages and limited the recovery of New Orleans.

NATIONAL POLITICS AND THE SOLID REPUBLICAN SOUTH

Katrina's breaking of the black-liberal political base in New Orleans is magnified by the likely loss of a congressional seat in

Louisiana in 2010. Though many of the local and state constraints on recovery might be overcome by an effective FEMA recovery plan, the agency can tilt Louisiana's political power in favor of Republicans simply by doing nothing. But FEMA has done something: early on it urged New Orleans residents to resettle in other states, especially in Houston;[10] its slow acquisition of trailers for redevelopment villages effectively prevented New Orleanians from returning to Louisiana; and it has actively resisted efforts of New Orleans and Louisiana officials to locate and contact their constituents, citing privacy concerns.[11]

FEMA's actions in the months after the storm must be viewed in the context of the administration's desperate effort to ensure that blame for the handling of the disaster lay with the state. In this regard they seem to have been successful. A Southern Media and Opinion Research poll showed a slight rise in the president's approval ratings among Louisianians three months after the storm. While the president's approval among black Louisianians dropped, it was offset by a rise among white respondents for a negligible overall gain. On the other hand, Governor Blanco's ratings dropped more than twenty points, and she lost support among all groups.[12]

Beyond the blame game, the administration sees an opportunity to destroy the last bastion of Democratic resistance in the "Solid South." Not only is Governor Blanco vulnerable in the elections two years from now, but Senator Landrieu and Congressman Charlie Melancon are seen as targets as well. Beyond Blanco's poor performance and Landrieu's early celebration of FEMA's response, both are vulnerable because of the loss of black voters in New Orleans. Melancon is not so vulnerable but will be the target of a concerted effort to unseat him so that, when districts are redrawn, the congressman south of New Orleans will be Republican (like in the seat to the north), guaranteeing that the current majority-black Orleans Parish–based district will be redrawn to the advantage of Republicans.

For Republicans, the storm has created a tremendous political opportunity that can be exploited while doing nothing more than pursuing the party's existing ideological opposition to governmental solutions and central planning. Having ensured that Governor Blanco is blamed for the evacuation catastrophe, the administration began in January to abandon its redevelopment promises. In rejecting the Baker bill, which would have financed the purchase of destroyed homes and cleared the way for large-scale redevelopment, the administration has argued that it has spent enough, that Louisiana cannot be trusted, and that by comparison, Republican-led Mississippi has done well with less.[13] This approach embraces individual landowner-based redevelopment, blames Louisiana's Democrats for any redevelopment failings, and ensures a less black New Orleans.

LIMITS OF BLACK POLITICS

Race politics is not an occasional deviation from "normal" politics, the consequence of someone *playing* the race card, but an entrenched condition of American political life. Americans tend to deny this, seeing race as interjected into normal politics by Katrina-like catastrophes or by self-serving politicians. In this context, black politics has retreated to the symbolic realm, focusing on locating "leaders," demanding apologies, and seeking "candid" conversations about race. This symbolic racial politics risks fatalism and defeatism in the face of leadership disappointments from the likes of Mayors Holden and Nagin and vigorous denials of any role of race in these "racial" catastrophes. But such analyses ignore the racialized political conditions that had already made Holden and Nagin poor defenders of black political interests, and especially of the interests of New Orleans's displaced working poor.

Holden and Nagin represent a new wave of black politicians who seem to prove the ability of black voters to elect candidates in the "influence" districts recently legitimated in the Supreme Court's reapportionment decisions. Mayor Holden was elected mayor of majority-black Baton Rouge, but in a bizarre city-parish government system that permits parishwide voting for mayor because he is also parish president. Consequently, Holden was elected in a classic influence district where black voters represented less than half of the electorate. Though Holden cast his election as a victory for black voters, he was elected by an overlapping coalition of black, progressive, and business-oriented voters. Holden's statements in the Katrina crisis illustrate the limits of this kind of coalition. Confident of black and progressive support, Holden was pushed to comfort the racist elements of the electorate to burnish his image as a "nonracial" mayor, to combat a presumption that he was "biased" for black citizens, and to reassure that he would defend the city from criminal evacuees. He was driven to validate stereotypes of black New Orleanians in order to head off an alternative coalition anchored by racist white voters. Holden thus lent his black identity to proving that rumors of mayhem were both true and "nonracial."

Though mayor of an overwhelmingly black city, Nagin was elected by a coalition of white voters and an "influence proportion" of black voters, defeating a candidate from the black political establishment. Nagin rode a generational shift in New Orleans politics that saw several incumbents replaced by young, highly educated black candidates from the city's middle class. The older Nagin was not part of this group and was an underdog candidate to make the runoff, but he benefited from the spirit of change, and when he did make the runoff, he won easily. Mayor Nagin is best seen as the latest in a succession of "ethnic" challengers to the city's "Creole"-black political elite. Previous challengers were liberal white-ethnic candidates, associated with the city's white business elites. They all failed, but Nagin, a conservative black businessman, succeeded because he forged a shaky alliance among mostly poor black voters who wanted change, white conservative voters, and voters who saw him as business friendly. This weak alliance produced unremarkable governance but good approval of Nagin until the storm led white voters to abandon him and speculate openly about which white candidate could win in the "new" New Orleans.[14] When he told a Martin Luther King Day gathering that the rebuilt city "will be chocolate at the end of the day," he was lambasted as a racist and his fate was sealed.[15]

Mayor Nagin's weak political position was obscured by the symbolic politics of the storm. Some saw his outbursts during the evacuation as a rare occasion for black pride. His "no-bullshit" style, calling the federal government out for ignoring his citizens, was taken by some as an example of an attractive "black" leadership manner in the midst of incompetence. Despite this attractive symbolism, two days after his outburst about no more press conferences, he stood dutifully at the president's press conference, lending the incompetent federal response legitimacy against the state's similarly incompetent efforts.

Mayor Nagin's contradictory race leadership symbolism is rooted in his fealty to the business elites of his coalition at the expense of his poor black coalition members. Nagin might already have been realigning his coalition before the storm, if one believes the critics of his police department's efforts to rein in second-line parades and of a police raid on the St. Joseph's Day celebration held by the city's "Mardi Gras Indians" in June. The black "Indians," who have masked and gathered for the Catholic holiday and Mardi Gras for over one hundred years, and the second-liners of the poor neighborhoods are central to the city's tourist image. So it was reasonable to see a Nagin-led class war emerging against the working poor that had helped elect him, in an empty symbolic gesture at addressing the city's epidemic crime. Indeed, class conflict might be the main product and appeal of symbolic racial politics. The widespread expression of solidarity with and sympathy for New Orleans evacuees was conspicuously absent just two months before Katrina when black tourists, in the city for the annual Essence Music Festival, were asked to boycott Bourbon Street bars. Though testers had shown that Bourbon Street bars were discriminating against black patrons, the middle-class black tourists defied the boycott. Black citizens and officials are as capable as anyone of a metaphorical solidarity with the poor, while demonizing them and holding them responsible for disasters, man-made and natural, when the costs are high.

Katrina produced a potent symbol of race inequality, but one of questionable value. Symbolic race politics is attractive because it permits discussion of race inequality in today's political environment, where any discussion of race is viewed as the product of "playing the race card," even racist. But symbolic politics tends to obscure the real background role of race, while the open interpretation it permits leads nowhere. Instead of easy symbolic interpretation, we ought to focus on precise ways in which race is used to obscure a vicious class warfare, the costs of which are borne by the poor *and* by black Americans. Until then, no amount of symbolic interpretation or racial disassociation will free black Americans from the curse of race. For now, black Americans ought take the ruins of New Orleans as (symbolically) representative of their own broken dreams of being real and influential participants in America's democratic project.

NOTES

1. "True Crime: Baton Rouge Embarrassed Itself by Believing Rumors About New Orleans Evacuees' Committing Crimes. But Public Safety Is a Real Issue," *Baton Rouge Business Report,* print edition, September 13, 2005. This statement was made by Holden's chief administrative officer, Walter Monsur, on Thursday, September 1, 2005.
2. Ibid.
3. Ibid.
4. Marie-Claire Guillard, Bureau of Labor Statistics Monthly Labor Reports: Proportions of Workers in Selected Pay Ranges, by Region and State (2003).
5. See www.livingwagecampaign.org, citing study of Robert Pollin, Stephanie Luce, and Mark Brenner of the University of Massachusetts, Amherst.
6. Liane Hansen, "Businesses Battle Back in Terrebonne Parish," *Weekend Edition,* National Public Radio; December 11, 2005.
7. "More Than 87% of New Orleans' Inner City Residents Were Employed Prior to Katrina, ICIC Study Reveals," press release, www.icic.org, September 19, 2005.
8. Katharine Donato and Shirin Hakimzadec, "The Changing Face of the Gulf Coast: Immigration to Louisiana, Mississippi, and Alabama," Migration Information Source of the Migration Policy Institute, www.migratioinformation.org/feature, January 1, 2006.

9. Kevin McGill, "FEMA Says Politics Delays Trailers: Chief Says Mobile Homes Ready, Waiting to Be Allowed into Cities," www.2theadvicate.com/cgi-bin/printme.pl, December 19, 2005.

10. Emily Kern, "Relocation out of Louisiana Proposed: FEMA Suggests Some Residents Leave Temporarily," *Baton Rouge Advocate,* December 19, 2005.

11. John Pomfort, "FEMA Restricts Evacuee Data, Citing Privacy," *Washington Post,* October 12, 2005.

12. See Robert Travis Scott, "Dive in Blanco's Popularity Reflected in Post-Storm Poll: Vitter rises; Landrieu and Bush Stand Pat," *New Orleans Times Picayune,* November 30, 2005

13. Gerald Shields and Michelle Millhollon, "Bush: $85 Billion Is Enough. President Explains Baker Bill Rejection," *Baton Rouge Advocate,* January 27, 2006.

14. See Robert Travis Scott, "Dive in Blanco's Popularity," suggesting in November that Nagin could place fifth in an open primary.

15. John Pope, "Evoking King, Nagin Calls New Orleans 'Chocolate City,' " *New Orleans Times Picayune,* January 17, 2006.

4.

THE *REAL* DIVIDE
Adolph L. Reed Jr.

In the context of Hurricane Katrina, race is a cheap and safely predictable alternative to pressing a substantive critique of the sources of the horror in New Orleans and its likely outcomes. Granted, the images projected from the Superdome, the convention center, overpasses, and rooftops seemed to cry out a stark statement of racial inequality. But that's partly because in the contemporary United States, race is the most familiar language of inequality or injustice. It's what we see partly because it's what we're accustomed to seeing, what we look for. Class—as income, wealth, and access to material resources, including a safety net of social connections—was certainly a better predictor than race of who evacuated the city before the hurricane, who was able to survive the storm itself, who was warehoused in the Superdome or convention center or stuck without food and water on the parched overpasses, who is marooned in shelters in Houston or elsewhere, and whose interests will be factored into the reconstruction of the city, who will be able to return.

New Orleans is a predominantly black city, and it is a largely poor city. The black population is disproportionately poor, and the poor population is disproportionately black. It is not surprising that those who were stranded and forgotten, probably those who died, were conspicuously black and poor. None of that, however, means that race—or even racism—is adequate as an explanation of those patterns of inequality. And race is especially useless as a basis on which to craft a politics that can effectively pursue social justice.

Before the "yes, buts" begin, I am not claiming that systematic inequalities in the United States are not significantly racialized. The evidence of racial disparities is far too great for any sane or honest person to deny, and they largely emerge from a history of discrimination and racial injustice. Nor am I saying that we should overlook that fact in the interest of some idealized nonracial or postracial politics.

Let me be blunter than I've ever been in print about what I am saying: As a political strategy, exposing racism is wrongheaded and at best an utter waste of time. It is the political equivalent of an appendix: a useless vestige of an earlier evolutionary moment that's usually innocuous but can flare up and become harmful.

There are two reasons for this judgment.

One is that the language of race and racism is too imprecise to describe effectively even how patterns of injustice and inequality are racialized in a post–Jim Crow world. "Racism" can cover everything from individual prejudice and bigotry, to unself-conscious perception of racial stereotypes, to concerted group action to exclude or subordinate, to the results of ostensibly neutral market forces.

It can be a one-word description and explanation of patterns of unequal distribution of income and wealth, services and opportunities, police brutality, a stockbroker's inability to get a cab, neighborhood dislocation and gentrification, poverty, unfair criticism of black or Latino athletes, or being denied admission to a boutique.

Because the category is so porous, it doesn't really explain anything. Indeed, it is an alternative to explanation.

Exposing racism apparently makes those who do it feel good about themselves. Doing so is cathartic, though safely so, in the same way that proclaiming one's patriotism is in other circles.

It is a summary, concluding judgment rather than a preliminary to a concrete argument. It doesn't allow for politically significant distinctions; in fact, as a strategy, exposing racism requires subordinating the discrete features of a political situation to the overarching goal of asserting the persistence and power of racism as an abstraction.

This leads to the second reason for my harsh judgment. Many liberals gravitate to the language of racism not simply because it makes them feel righteous but also because it doesn't carry any political warrant beyond exhorting people not to be racist. In fact, it often is exactly the opposite of a call to action. Such formulations as "racism is our national disease" or similar pieties imply that racism is a natural condition. Further, it implies that most whites inevitably and immutably oppose blacks and therefore can't be expected to align with them around common political goals.

This view dovetails nicely with Democrats' contention that the only way to win elections is to reject a social justice agenda that is stigmatized by association with blacks and appeal to an upper-income white constituency concerned exclusively with issues like abortion rights and the deficit.

Upper-status liberals are more likely to have relatively secure, rewarding jobs, access to health care, adequate housing, and prospects for providing for the kids' education, and are much less likely to be in danger of seeing their nineteen-year-old go off to Iraq. They tend, therefore, to have a higher threshold of tolerance for political compromise in the name of electing this year's sorry procorporate Democrat. Acknowledging racism—and, of course, being prochoice—is one of the few ways many of them can distinguish themselves from their Republican co-workers and relatives.

As the appendix analogy suggests, insistence on understanding inequality in racial terms is a vestige of an earlier political style. The race line persists partly out of habit and partly because it connects with the material interests of those who would be race-relations technicians. In this sense, race is not an alternative to class. The tendency to insist on the primary of race itself stems from a class perspective.

For roughly a generation it seemed reasonable to expect that defining inequalities in racial terms would provoke some, albeit inadequate, remedial response from the federal government. But that's no longer the case; nor has it been for quite some time. That approach presumed a federal government that was concerned at least not to appear racially unjust. Such a government no longer exists.

A key marker of the right's victory in national politics is that the discussion of race now largely serves as a way to reinforce a message to whites that the public sector is there merely to help some combination of black, poor, and loser. Liberals have legitimized this perspective through their own racial bad faith. For many whites, the discussion of race also reinforces the idea that cutting public spending is justifiably aimed at weaning a lazy black underclass off the dole or—in the supposedly benign, liberal Democratic version—teaching them "personal responsibility."

New Orleans is instructive. The right has a built-in counter to the racism charge by mobilizing all the scurrilous racial stereotypes that it has propagated to justify attacks on social protection and government responsibility all along. Only those who already are inclined to believe that racism is the source of inequality accept that charge. For others, nasty victim-blaming narratives abound to explain away obvious racial disparities.

What we must do, to pursue justice for displaced, impoverished New Orleanians as well as for the society as a whole, is to emphasize that their plight is a more extreme, condensed version of the precarious position of millions of Americans today, as more and more lose health care, bankruptcy protection, secure employment, affordable housing, civil liberties, and access to education. And their plight will be the future of many, many more people in this country once the bipartisan neoliberal consensus reduces government to a tool of corporations and the investor class alone.

Part Three

DISASTERS AND DIASPORA

5.

HISTORICIZING KATRINA
Clement Alexander Price

Like a fire bell in the night, to use Thomas Jefferson's words when he learned of the frightening debate over the Missouri Compromise, many Americans were awakened by the social destruction wrought by Hurricane Katrina when it swept across the Gulf, making landfall on Louisiana, Mississippi, Alabama, and Florida in the late summer of 2005. The storm's aftermath has brought into high relief the enduring fault lines of race, class, and generation. During the first few days of the disaster, electronic and print media provided stark images and testimony of thousands of colored citizens trying to escape cities and towns under water. Indeed, the media actually contributed to the racialized way in which Americans view black people, especially those in trouble and in need of aid. Early on in the crisis, poor blacks were curiously referred to as "refugees" in the media, as if they were from another country. When blacks sought to find food and other essentials after it became clear that assistance was not on the way, they were quickly viewed as looters and common criminals. Through a different lens such behavior by whites was viewed quite differently: they were seeking to survive the aftermath of the storm. As astonished Americans saw the ill fortune shouldered by poor black people in New Orleans, and as far too many of them seemed surprised that modern race relations was implicated in the disaster wrought by Katrina, historians are reminded of an America where natural destruction, social collapse, and sadness have been racialized.

Natural disasters in the United States provide a complicated context in which race and racism can be discussed anew. Indeed, although Hurricane Katrina is being exceptionalized as the nation's worst, the social aftermath of the storm is hardly without precedent. The wrath of the natural world, and the seemingly complicit role of powerful leaders on the national and local level, is a part of the nation's history and memory.

More than a century ago, in 1900, the infamous flood in Galveston, Texas, left thousands of residents and settlers vulnerable to water, disease, and the absence of a plan to save lives. The death toll may have been as high as 8,000. Many of the vulnerable ones were blacks at the mercy of a social hierarchy that placed them at or near the bottom. The plight of those who survived has been all but obscured by the timing of their ill fate. The public sphere, as we know it, had not been fully formed. Blacks, Mexicans, poor folks generally, were not given the kind of attention we have become accustomed to. They were all but invisible.

The years that followed the Galveston flood and the other disasters of the early twentieth century—including boll weevil infestation and flooding in the Gulf States—set the stage for the greatest demographic shift of blacks since the last decades of the Trans-Atlantic slave trade, the so-called Great Migration. For years Americans have seen that shift through a rather exceptional lens: Southern blacks, the progeny of slaves, moved out of the South in an attempt to move up. It has been at the center of the modern black narrative, involving countless families, including my own, and the logical place to begin any discussion of black American life. The rise of concentrated black communities in the North, Mid-West and Far West, we have long believed, was the part of the push-and-pull dynamic that simultaneously encouraged blacks to leave the homesteads of their forebears and try life anew, as many migrants said, in "northern country."

Fast forwarding to Katrina, we might want to reconsider how the pervasiveness of natural disasters influenced the way modern and contemporary black life unfolded. Perhaps the unpredictability of nature's wrath should be factored into our perception of the American past, when blacks seem to be disproportionately vulnerable, when they are buffeted by the winds, the waters, and public indifference. Recent scholarship does indeed suggest that poor people are disproportionately at greater risk during disastrous episodes like hurricanes and floods, are less prepared when disaster strikes, and face greater destruction to home and hearth when compared to those with more substantial means.

The last century's most devastating natural disasters were preludes to what we grimly witnessed when Katrina hit and when its aftermath intersected with race, class, and human indifference to the proper stewardship of land and water. That natural disaster brought into high relief the ebb and flow of American race relations and the vulnerability of black Americans when their private lives rely on public response. Many have left their destroyed homes and communities, probably never to return as residents.

It is a sad reality that the public sphere, which African Americans have long sought to ennoble and empower as the common ground for equality and justice, continues to be racialized against the individual and collective interests of black and brown citizens of the Republic. Such is Katrina's legacy, and the legacy of race when storms and other destructive natural forces hit areas where black communities exist all too poorly.

6.

GREAT MIGRATIONS?
Michael Eric Dyson

In the aftermath of Hurricane Katrina, black folk in the Gulf Coast faced the cruel reality of yet another "storm-induced diaspora."[1] Earlier storms, especially the Great Mississippi Flood of 1927, had flushed back Americans from their homes in search of relief from the desperate poverty and brutal racism that the disaster revealed. But this most recent tragedy harkened back even further: the deadly waters of slavery's middle passage flooded the black collective memory. One of the unifying themes of slavery and storms in the black imagination is the traumatic dispersal of black folk across rugged, even resistant, geographies. Black folk have built communities in the most hostile conditions imaginable. They have beat back both natural and man-made disasters to stake bold claims of citizenship and common humanity.

Of course, black folk have, over the centuries, endured various qualities and versions of dispersion, including the familiar migrations blacks have undertaken or been forced into. Apart from slavery, perhaps the most memorable exodus of black folk is the Great Migration that stretched from the early twentieth century into the 1930s, as blacks shirked their rural southern roots to embrace northern urban life. To be sure, the Great Migration is a complex story of forces that pushed and pulled blacks from their native haunts—southern white blacklash after Reconstruction; the decline of southern agrarian capitalism; and the lure of northern economic opportunity in a region whose landscape was not as violently marked by the visible signposts of white supremacy.

But migration is also never merely physical and spatial. It also involves political, psychic, social, and spiritual forces that affect the shape and duration of black diaspora. Neither is migration a static process. Rather, it is dynamic, fluid and evolutionary, unfolding in both layers of dispersal and various points of entry into, and exit from, the diasporic identity. The restless black quest for home suggests the search for common roots with other citizens. It also points to an unquenchable desire for a unique black identity forged in the give and take of black comings and goings in the world.

If black migrations don't stay put and measure both the kick in the pants and the tug of dreams that motivate black movement, they also aren't simple phenomena that can be explained by single theories of mobility. Among many others, there are at least three kinds of movement that Hurricane Katrina revealed: submerged, subversive, and subsidized migrations. How these play out will say a lot about how black folk will wake from this latest racial and economic nightmare.

Submerged migrations occur when there is a shift in concentrations of population within specific geographical regions. More particularly, such internal migrations count as submerged migrations when minority populations are economically dislocated, socially displaced, and spatially segregated. Thus, folk are shifted within, or immediately outside of, cities in the effort to protect wealthier communities (as with Chicago project dwellings like Cabrini Green being dismantled, and their populations displaced from the wealthy Gold Coast area); to physically quarantine poor populations in working class exurbs to make room for the production of entrepreneurial projects (such as the building of sports stadiums); the construction of new highways; or the development of new properties.

Submerged migrations are also sparked, and exacerbated, by shifts in the political economy and in urban geography and demography that have a negative impact on poor black people. The shift from manufacturing to high-end service industries drives millions of workers to the bottom of the economy. In this pivotal transitional moment in the economy, high-tech, knowledge-based jobs proliferate while low-wage jobs in the service sector are occupied by the working poor. Furthermore, the gentrification of poor, mixed-wage neighborhoods by upwardly mobile professionals weakens the already fragile hold of working poor households on economic stability. The possibility of homeownership is almost nil in such communities among the lower classes, and access to rental homes is nearly impossible. Thus, the poor are forced into bleaker neighborhoods with little capital concentration, entrepreneurial energy, or upward mobility. This is the doorway into one of the most vicious aspects of submerged migration—concentrated poverty, which leads to poor homes, communities, jobs, and education, all of which produce more material deprivation and social suffering.

New Orleans has suffered the lethal consequences of the submerged migration of black populations for decades. Some middle-class blacks, and many more working-class and working poor blacks, have been concentrated in the city's Ninth Ward for several decades. As New Orleans city council member Cynthia Willard-Lewis told me in an interview, the Ninth Ward is "a community with many economic challenges—chronic and systemic poverty in a core group. However, there are many families, also, that are middle class and own multiple properties, have professional backgrounds, and have educated their children. And because of the roots, the fact that mama and grandmamma and daughters all live in the same neighborhood, there's a real connectivity of home and family. It's a diversity of income, but the greater portion, because of the challenge of poverty and the fact that the elderly population primarily has fixed incomes. The numbers are lower on the economic street, but higher on the home-owner street."

The linchpin to submerged migration of the poor is chronic under education. As Willard-Lewis further explained, poor education worsens the effects of concentrated poverty and extends its reach into every area of black life.

> There are many challenges with the public systems that provide resources and services to the poor—our public education, first and foremost. And the fact that all of those things that provide for quality education were lacking, from oversized classrooms, lack of resources, stressed teachers, poor infrastructure, crumbling buildings, limited extracurricular activities—all of those things that work against children having the right to great educational opportunities, which then open doors to a future where they can earn significant wages, were in limited access in New Orleans. So you will probably have . . . high illiteracy rates and high drop out rates. In addition to that, the standardized test-taking experiences, which forced many of the children out of the classroom because they knew they couldn't pass those tests. . . . So there were many barriers and requirements that the children had to jump through when

they went through the door of a crumbling old school without books in an overcrowded classroom, that didn't equip them and didn't speak to their emotional, spiritual, academic, physical needs. And the ravages of Katrina have hit all the systems: our health care system, our public education system, our law enforcement system. They're all now working under great burdens of rebuilding. And my hope is that Katrina presents an opportunity to really address what the needs of the people are as they have articulated them.

If submerged migrations drive poor people into poor neighborhoods through economic dislocation and social displacement, then *subversive migrations* disperse black folk across regional and national boundaries through both natural and social disasters. Subversive migrations occur when, for instance, storms or floods force black folk from their native regions into foreign territories— both within their nations and beyond—and when racist practices cause blacks to flee their homes. On the face of it, natural disaster is race-neutral, since its fury falls fiercely on all populations in a vulnerable region. But in New Orleans, the higher, safer ground has always been occupied by richer, whiter folk, while the lower, more dangerous ground, has always been the province of poorer people. That poor black people have been exiled to vulnerable territory suggests the racial politics of both demographic and geographical shifts and trends. It also points to the fact that while nature's fury may be color-blind, the consequences of such fury surely aren't, since they track the social and racial hierarchies of the cultures on which they light.

Many of the migrations undertaken by black folk have been in response to the vicious acts of white terror, violence, and dominance. As Steven Hahn argues, migration's political character could be clearly and painfully apparent, as in Grimes County, Texas, where the violent seizure of power by the White Man's Union in 1900 sparked an "exodus" of hundreds (perhaps one-third) of the black inhabitants. More commonly, the politics were to be found in smaller-scale rejections of the hardships, humiliations, and coercions that black migrants believed whites were determined to inflict on them and in the established institutions and social networks that were their vehicles of change.[2]

Moreover, traumatic events like the 1927 Great Flood of Mississippi reveal the racial hurricanes and cultural floods that are the cruel aftermath of natural disaster. When black folk were forcibly exiled from their homes in the Great Flood, they were subject to the naked aggression of the state as it imposed sanctions on black life that intensified the affects of the natural disaster. Black folk were herded into work camps where they were forced to rebuild ravaged regions without compensation. They were also denied both their citizenship rights and the right to occupy land and structures they had helped to restore and reconstruct. Their treatment during the Great Flood reflected broader trends in the treatment of blacks at the hands of whites: their formally organized towns were often the target of racial terror, including, most famously, the bombing of an all-black community in 1921 in Tulsa, Oklahoma; their places of recreation were resented and closed; and their families, especially their more vocal members, were run off and forced to seek refuge in safer corners of the black diaspora.

Subversive migrations thrive not only on the coercion of poor black populations into vulnerable geographies, but on the social chaos and racial disarray encouraged by the opportunistic exploitation of natural disaster for racist purposes. When, for instance, black folk were forced to work against their wills in the

Great Flood, whites were able to utilize black labor to their racial, and societal, advantage. Moreover, subversive migrations compound the oppression that spatial and psychic dislocation breeds. As Jesse Jackson argued in an interview with me, such forces shouldn't be confused with the planned and desired mobility that characterize migration.

> Dislocation, in the name of relocation, is not to be confused with migration. Blacks migrate of their own volition. Because it's more oppressive economically and militarily, blacks have been forced to rebuild at gunpoint. Here [in Katrina] people are put on planes for uncertain destinations and landing in Utah, or in California. This became an exile. I would distinguish between exile and migrations. To paraphrase the Bible, "They took us away, so we sat by the rivers of Babylon and there we wept." They took people away. They didn't migrate; they were taken away. Forcibly. In exile. And now, FEMA will not give the addresses to the State Board of Elections so they can get their voting material for the upcoming elections. They plan to keep them in exile so it'll affect the state's political demographics.

Jackson also detected in the subversive migration of black folk in Katrina a haunting echo of slavery.

> I saw people where their family was separated—men from women, children from the old and the sick from the well. And with no communication. They didn't know where others had gone, and they just began to panic in desperation. "Where's my wife? Where's my mother? Where's my child? Where's my daddy? What happened to our house?" They were, like, disoriented. It looked like the hull of a slave ship experience.

In the latest act of subversive migration, black folk have been dispersed over forty-four states in the nation, recalling the dreadful dispersal of their forbears during slavery. While Katrina may lack the explicitly racist overtones of earlier natural disasters, the undeniable racial consequences of the subversive migration of hundreds of thousands of blacks underscore persistent patterns of racial hierarchy in the nation.

Finally, *subsidized migrations* occur when black masses are drawn forth by the promise of work or a style of life that reflects an investment in black survival or a patronage of black skill and talent. It is widely known, of course, that poor black folk were drawn north away from their impoverished southern existence by the possibility of wage work that would adequately compensate blacks beyond the debt peonage of the sharecropper's plantation. Hence, northern industrialists subsidized black migration by offering fair pay for hard work, an offer that, in the context of black life, established a revolutionary predicate: that black workers were, in some ways, if not quite equal to white workers, then at least much further along the path to parity than in the south.

But it was not only the black poor who benefited from the push north. Recently historians have argued that the black elite were also lured north for greater professional opportunities and freedoms. As James Gregory contends, black professionals

> were leaving at very high rates, especially graduates of the Negro colleges who, unless they went into the ministry or teaching, had little chance of finding appropriate work in the South. Their numbers were small, but attorneys, social workers, writers, musicians, and other professionals along with merchants, preachers, and teachers were an important part of the Great Migration. When Asa Philip Randolph followed his thirst for education to New York in 1911, when William Dawson left Tennessee to study law in Chicago in 1915, when George Baker decided to move his ministry to

Brooklyn and call himself Father Divine, and when Bessie Smith and Louis Armstrong took their music north in the 1920s, they too were part of the Southern Diaspora and part of why it became such a momentous force in the reorganization of American society.[3]

Although Gregory highlights the intersecting racial interests of poor and middle-class blacks in a migration subsidized, in part, by northern economic and social forces, his argument also under-scores the fact that, even among blacks, there were, and are, parallel migrations. In Katrina, both racial and class elements con-verged in the subsidized migration of black folk. More well-to-do blacks, and whites, enjoyed an experience of evacuation signifi-cantly different from that of the black masses. As it turns out, the parallel migrations of the well-to-do and the worse-off are sharply distinct.

First, the poor were, and remain, dependent upon government to subsidize their exodus, while wealthier citizens had, and still have, independent means to subsidize their evacuation and migra-tion from New Orleans. Second, the more well-to-do are able to squeeze out greater advantage from their evacuations and migra-tions, either by finding work in locales away from New Orleans; in sustaining themselves through independent means; or in exploit-ing the tragedy through reconstruction and development con-tracts that subsidize their migration, and their repatriation to the city, in a far different manner than the poor. And third, the well-to-do have only been faced with temporary exiles, exoduses and mi-grations; the poor face permanent displacements, dislocations, and forced migrations. Although their evacuations-turned-permanent migrations are allegedly subsidized through federal government aid, the meager-to-modest payments most are able to draw down mean that the black poor face far more difficult circumstances even when their living situation has greatly improved.

The migrations of black folk reveal as much about the nation's response to black pain and suffering as they do about the self-determining mobility of the masses of blacks. Whether they are submerged, subversive, or subsidized, black migrations tell on the moral, political, and racial backdrop of black movement. Each meaning of migration showed up in the tragedy of Katrina, but only a future that we shape by our principled and determined action will reveal which element of black migration prevails.

NOTES

1. Dan Barry and Adam Nossiter, "Mardi Gras Set for City Stripped of All but Pride," *New York Times,* February 17, 2006.
2. Steven Hahn, *A Nation Under Our Feet: Black Political Struggles in the Rural South from Slavery to the Great Migration* (Cambridge, Massachusetts: the Belknap Press of Harvard University Press, 2003), 456–57.
3. James N. Gregory, *The Southern Diaspora: How the Great Migrations of Black and White Southerners Transformed America* (Chapel Hill: the University of North Carolina Press, 2005), 28.

Part Four

PERCEIVING THE IMAGE, FRAMING IDENTITY, AND CRITIQUING "CRIME"

7.

LOOT OR FIND: FACT OR FRAME?
Cheryl I. Harris and Devon W. Carbado

Both photographs by AP Photo/Dave Martin

A

B

EVIDENCE OF THINGS SEEN

What do these images represent? What facts do they convey? We could say that image A depicts a man who, in the aftermath of Katrina, is wading through high waters with food supplies and a big black plastic bag. We might say that image B depicts a man and woman, both wearing backpacks. They, too, are wading through high waters in the aftermath of Katrina, and the woman appears to be carrying food supplies.

This is not how these images were presented in the press. The captions that appeared with the two photos, both of which ran on Yahoo! news, were quite different. The caption for image A read: "A young man walks through chest-deep flood water after looting a grocery store in New Orleans." The caption for image B read: "Two residents wade through chest-deep waters after finding bread and soda from a local grocery store after Hurricane Katrina came through the area." The caption for image A, then, tells us that a crime has been committed; the caption for image B tells that a fierce, poignant struggle for survival is under way—the subjects have just found food. Image A depicts a young black man; image B shows a white man and woman.

The images and their respective captions almost immediately stirred up significant controversy. People complained that the captions accompanying the images were racially suggestive: black people "loot" and white people "find." *Boston Globe* correspondent Christina Pazzanese wondered, "I am curious how one photographer knew the food was looted by one but not the other. Were interviews conducted as they swam by?" [1]

Not everyone agreed, however, that the images and captions reflected a racial problem. As one commentator put it:

> It's difficult to draw any substantiated conclusions from these photos' captions. Although they were both carried by many news outlets, they were taken by two different photographers and came from two different services, the Associated Press (AP) and the Getty Images via Agence France-Presse (AFP). Services make different stylistic standards for how they caption photographs, or the dissimilar wordings may have been due to nothing more than the preferences

of different photographers and editors, or the difference might be the coincidental result of a desire to avoid repetitive wording (similar photographs from the same news services variously describe the depicted actions as "looting," "raiding," "taking," "finding," and "making off"). The viewer also isn't privy to the contexts in which the photographs were taken—it's possible that in one case the photographer actually saw his subject exiting an unattended grocery store with an armful of goods, while in the other case the photographer came upon his subjects with supplies in hand and could only make assumptions about how they obtained them.[2]

For the most part, this controversy focused on a question of fact. Did the black person really loot the goods he was carrying? Did the white man and white woman really find the food they were carrying? Indeed, the director of media relations at the Associated Press suggested that, as to image A, "he [the photographer] saw the person go into the shop and take the goods. . . . that's why he wrote 'looting' in the article."[3] In other words, the fact of the matter was that the black man in image A was a looter.

The photographer of image B, Chris Graythen, maintained,

I wrote the caption about the two people who "found" the items. I believed in my opinion, that they did simply find them, and not "looted" them in the definition of the word. The people were swimming in chest deep water, and there were other people in the water, both white and black. I looked for the best picture. There were a million items floating in the water—we were right near a grocery store that had 5+ feet of water in it. It had no doors. The water was moving, and the stuff was floating away. These people were not ducking into a store and busting down windows to get electronics. They picked up bread and Cokes that were floating in the water. They would have floated away anyhow.[4]

To some extent, the credibility of Grayther's explanation is beside the point here. That is, the loot-or-find problem of image A and image B cannot fully be addressed with reference to the individual intent of those who either took the picture or produced the accompanying interpretive text. Indeed, it is entirely plausible that had the photos appeared without any captions, they would have been read the same way.[5] This is because while neither "loot" nor "find" is written on either image, in the context of public disorder, the race of the subjects inscribes those meanings.

THE "COLOR-BLIND" FRAME

Drawing on facts about both Hurricane Katrina and the public's response to it, this chapter queries whether efforts to change the racial status quo and eliminate inequality should or can rely solely on facts or empiricism. There is a growing sense within the civil rights community that more empirical research is needed to persuade mainstream Americans that racism remains a problem in American society and that the elimination of racial disadvantage is not a do-it-yourself project. The idea seems to be that if only more Americans knew certain "facts" (for example, about the existence of implicit bias) they would be more inclined to support civil rights initiatives (for example, affirmative action). We agree that more empirical research is needed. Facts are important—indeed crucial—since so much of public opinion is grounded in misinformation. We simply do not think that there is a linear progression between raw empiricism and more enlightened public opinion about race and racism. Put another way, we do not believe that facts speak for themselves.

It is precisely the recognition that facts don't speak for them-

selves that helps to explain why scholars across academic fields and
politicians across the political spectrum continue to pay significant attention to the social and cognitive processes that shape how
we interpret facts. Of the variety of theories—in sociology, political science, law, anthropology, psychology, and economics—that
attempt to explain these processes, most share the idea that we interpret events through frames—interpretational structures that,
consciously and unconsciously, shape what we see and how we see
it. In the words of one scholar, framing refers to "understanding a
story you already know and saying, 'Oh yeah, that one.' "[6] As we
process and make sense of an event, we take account of and simultaneously ignore facts that do not fit the frame, and sometimes we
supply ones that are missing. Thus, it is sometimes said that
"frames trump facts."[7]

The most relevant and dominant frame is color blindness, or
the belief that race is *not* a factor in how we make sense of the
world. Color blindness is a kind of metaframe that comprises three
interwoven racial scripts: (1) because of *Brown v. Board of Education* and the civil rights reforms it inaugurated, racism is by and
large a thing of the past; (2) when racism does rear its ugly head, it
is the product of misguided and irrational behavior on the part of
self-declared racial bigots, who are few and far between; and (3)
racial consciousness—whether in the form of affirmative action or
Jim Crow–like racism—should be treated with suspicion, if not re-
jected outright. The gradual ascendancy and eventual racial dominance of color blindness frames the facts of racial inequality
(manifested, for example, in disparities in wealth and educational
outcomes between blacks and whites) as a function of something
other than racism. Because scientists have largely repudiated the
notion of biological inferiority, color blindness frames the prob-

lem of racial disadvantage in terms of conduct. The problem is not genes but culture, not blood but behavior: were black people to engage in normatively appropriate cultural practices—work hard, attend school, avoid drugs, resist crime—they would transcend their current social status and become part of the truly advantaged. On this view, black disadvantage is both expected and deserved—a kind of natural disaster not produced by racism.

At least initially, Katrina challenged the supremacy of color blindness. The tidal wave of suffering that washed over New Orleans seemed incontrovertible evidence of the salience of race in contemporary U.S. society.[8] The simple fact that the faces of those left to fend for themselves or die were overwhelmingly black raised questions about the explanatory power of color blindness under which race is deemed irrelevant.[9] Racial suffering was everywhere. And black people were dying—prime time live. One had to close one's eyes, or willfully blind oneself, not to see this racial disaster. Everyone, it seemed, except government officials, was riveted. And there was little disagreement that Katrina exposed shameful fissures in America's social fabric; that the precipitating event was an act of God, not the cultural pathology of the victims; and that the government's response, at least in the initial phases, was woefully inadequate. Seasoned mainstream journalists wept and railed, while ordinary Americans flooded relief organizations with money.

The tragedy of Katrina created a rupture in the racial-progress narrative that had all but erased the suffering of poor black people from the political landscape. In contrast to the pre-Katrina picture, black people were perceived to be innocent victims. Black people were perceived to have a legitimate claim on the nation-state. Black people were perceived to be deserving of government help. Katrina—or the *facts* the public observed about its effects—disrupted our tendency to *frame* black disadvantage in terms of cultural deficiency. But how did that happen? And doesn't this disruption undermine our central point about facts and frames?

Not at all. Frames are not static. Epic events like Katrina push up against and can temporarily displace them. All those people. All that suffering. This can't be America. How could we let this happen? That question—how could we let this happen?—reflected a genuine humanitarian concern for fellow human beings. Moreover, the compelling facts about Katrina raised a number of questions about racial inequality previously suppressed under color blindness. Indeed, as the humanitarian crisis peaked with the retreating floodwaters, a debate over the role of race in the disaster quickly emerged. The unrelenting spectacle of black suffering bodies demanded an explanation. Why were those New Orleans residents who remained trapped during Katrina largely black and poor? Was it, as hip-hop artist Kanye West argued, a case of presidential indifference to, or dislike of, poor black people?[10] Or was it, as Ward Connerly asserted, the predictable consequence of a natural disaster that befell a city that just happened to be predominantly black? Was it, as Linda Chavez claimed, the result of a culture of dependency combined with local bureaucratic incompetence? Was race a factor in determining who survived and who did not?[11] Or did class provide a better explanation?[12] Finally, could we ever fully understand Katrina without meaningfully engaging the legacy of slavery?[13] These and other, similar questions were pushed into the foreground by the force of Katrina's devastation.

But the frame of color blindness did not disappear. It manifested itself in the racial divide that emerged with respect to how people answered the foregoing questions. While there is some intraracial diversity of opinion among public figures about the role of race and racism in explaining what happened, there remains a striking racial difference in how the disaster is viewed. According to public opinion polls, whites largely reject the notion that race explains the governmental disregard, while blacks assert that the fact that the victims were black and poor was a significant part of the story.[14] This difference over the difference that race makes reflects competing racial frames. Thus, while the facts of what happened in Katrina's aftermath unsettled the familiar color-blind racial script that poor black people were the authors of their own plight, those facts did not ultimately displace core ideas embedded in the color-blind frame: race is irrelevant and racism largely does not exist. Most whites were able to see black people as victims, but they were unwilling to link their victim status to race or racism. A more acceptable story was that black people in New Orleans suffered only because of bureaucratic inefficiencies in the wake of a natural disaster. Race simply could not be a factor. Katrina then only partially destabilized the frame of color blindness. To the extent that our starting point for thinking about race is that it does not matter, other racial frames or scripts more easily fit within the overarching frame. These frames can both explicitly invoke race and, even more powerfully, implicitly play the race card. After the initial uncertainty, what emerged in the wake of Katrina was the frame of "law and order"—a racial script that permeated the debate over the iconic photographs with which we began our essay, and over the post-Katrina relief efforts. The media were both author and reader of events in ways that both challenged and underwrote this racial frame.

A PICTURE IS WORTH A THOUSAND WORDS

Recall Chris Grayther's response to the racial controversy concerning the images with which we began this chapter. With regard to image B, Grayther asserted that he "looked for the best picture." More specifically, Grayther searched for an image that would best narrate a particular factual story: that people were wading through water to find food. According to Grayther, both whites and blacks were finding food in the chest-high water. Unlike pre-Katrina New Orleans, this space was racially integrated. Grayther searched this racially integrated body of water for a picture that would most successfully convey the idea of people finding food (as distinct from people "ducking into a store and busting down windows to get electronics"). Grayther's "best picture"—his "Oh yeah, that one"—emerged when he saw the two white people photographed in image B. Their images best fit the caption that Grayther already had in mind, people wading through water to find food. Because people are more likely to associate blacks with looting ("ducking into a store and busting down windows to get electronics") than with finding food, Grayther's selection makes sense. Indeed, one can infer from Grayther's decision to photograph white people that it was easier to frame white people as despondent people finding food than it was to frame black people in that way. To put the point slightly differently, there would be some dissonance between the image of black people in those high waters and a caption describing people finding food. This dissonance is not about facts—whether in fact the black people were finding food; the dissonance is about frames—the racial association between black people and looting, particularly on the heels of a natural disaster or social upheaval.

Two caveats before moving on. First, nothing above is intended to suggest that Grayther's decision to photograph the two white people was racially conscious—that is, intentionally motivated by race. Frames operate both consciously and unconsciously; his selection of whites to photograph (and his "natural selection" against blacks) converged with existing racial frames about criminality and perpetrators, on the one hand, and law-abidingness and victims, on the other. The two photos were perfect mirror images of each other. But only image B could convey a story of survival against adversity; image A was inconsistent with that script. The presence of a black man with a big plastic bag in the context of a natural disaster is already inscribed with meaning. In that sense, the black man in image A did not require a caption to be framed; nor did the white man and woman in image B. The stereotype of black criminality was activated by image A and the many images like it, which showed the central problem in New Orleans not to be the lack of humanitarian aid, but the lack of law and order.

The second caveat: our analysis should not be read as an argument against empiricism or a claim that facts are irrelevant. We simply mean to say that racial frames shape our perceptions of the facts. This does not mean that we are overdetermined by frames or that we are unable to escape their interpretative strictures. Rather, the point is that dependence on "just the facts" will seldom be enough to dislodge racial frames.[15] Partly this is because racial frames are installed not as the result of empiricism, but in spite of it. Consider color blindness. It is the dominant racial frame for understanding race not because of facts but because of a well-financed political project to entrench and naturalize a color-blind understanding of American race relations.[16] Accordingly, something more than facts is required to undo the racial work color blindness continues to perform; and something more than facts is required to dislodge the normativity of color blindness itself.

FROM RESCUE TO OCCUPATION: SEEING THE INVISIBLE

I'd rather have them here dead than alive. And at least they're not robbing you and you [don't] have to worry about feeding them.[17]
—A resident of St. Gabriel when asked for her reactions to the decision to designate the town as a collective morgue

To the extent that our discussion of the problem of racial frames has largely examined representational issues, one mighty reasonably ask: What are the material consequences of this problem? And how, if at all, did it injure black New Orleanians in the wake of Hurricane Katrina? The answer relates to two interconnected frames: the frame of law and order and the frame of black criminality. Working together, these frames rendered black New Orleanians dangerous, unprotectable, and unrescuable.

In the immediate aftermath of Katrina, the media pointedly criticized the slow pace at which the federal government was responding to the disaster. But the critical stance was short-lived and quickly gave way to a focus on the breakdown of law and order, a frame that activated a familiar stereotype about black criminality. While initially blacks were seen as victims of Hurricane Katrina and a failed governmental response, this victim status proved to be highly unstable. Implicit in the frame that "this can't be America" is the notion that the neglect in the wake of Katrina was a violation of the duty of care owed to all citizens of the nation. This social contract includes blacks as citizens; and indeed the claim by blacks,

"We are American"—a statement vigorously asserted by those contained in the convention center[18]—responded to and relied upon that frame.[19]

As time progressed, the social currency of the image of blacks as citizens of the state to whom a duty of care is owed diminished. It rubbed uneasily against the more familiar racial framing of poor black people as lazy, undeserving, and inherently criminal. Concern over the looting of property gradually took precedence over the humanitarian question of when people might be rescued and taken off of the highways and rooftops. Thus, while armed white men were presumed to be defending their property, black men with guns constituted gangs of violent looters who had to be contained. Under this frame, the surrounding towns and parishes that constituted potential refuge for black New Orleans residents who had no means to evacuate before the storm became no-go areas because of concerns about black criminality.

A particularly stark example of this came during the CNN interview on September 8 between Christiane Amanpour and the resident of St. Gabriel quoted above. The sentiment that dead blacks were better than live ones was enforced not only by local authorities who, like the Gretna police, turned people away at gunpoint, but by the National Guard and other local authorities who purpotedly denied the Red Cross permission to enter the city shortly after the storm because of concerns about the safety of the rescuers.[20]

These fears were grounded in what ultimately proved to be grossly exaggerated or completely unsubstantiated media accounts of violence and attacks particularly in the Superdome and the convention center.[21] The tone of these reports were hyperbolic, evoking all of the familiar racial subtexts: FOX News, for example, issued a news report the day before the Superdome was evacuated that "there were many reports of robberies, rapes, car-jackings, rioters and murder and that violent gangs are roaming the streets at night, hidden by the cover of darkness." The *Los Angeles Times* was no less sensational, reporting that National Guard troops had to take rooftop positions to scan for snipers and armed mobs as gunfire rang out.[22] These reports were taken as authoritative by police and other law enforcement officials. Indeed, even the mayor of the city, Ray Nagin, who is black, spoke of "hundreds of armed gang members" killing and raping people inside the Superdome, such that the crowd had descended to an "almost animalistic state."[23]

We are not arguing that there was no violence. There was. But the frames of black criminality and law and order overdetermined how we interpreted both the extent and nature of that violence. For example, consider how the "facts" about rape were interpreted and discussed. Recently, advocacy groups for victims of sexual assault have begun to challenge the official count of reported rapes—four—as unrealistically low. A national database newly created by the National Sexual Violence Resource Center reports more than forty sexual assaults, while another victim's rights organization has reported more than 150 post-Katrina violent crimes, of which about one-third were sexual assaults, including those committed in the homes of host families.[24] This suggests that reports of sexual assaults were underreported. Paradoxically, at the same time that reports of rape were cited to confirm stereotypes of black criminality, the black women victims of *actual* rapes suffered an unconscionable degree of official disregard. While accounts of rape were invoked as signs of the disintegration of social order in New Orleans, some of the black women who experienced sexual violence were unable to file reports with law enforcement officials despite their efforts to do so, notwithstanding the city's ostensible mission to maintain law and order to protect victims from crime.

One of the more prominent examples of this official disregard was Charmaine Neville, a member of the family of renowned New Orleans musicians, who was raped by a roving group of men who invaded her community in the Lower Ninth Ward while she and her neighbors struggled unsuccessfully over a series of days to be evacuated and to obtain medical care.[25] Neville's searing account of what happened to her is a clear indictment of the government for its neglect: "What I want people to understand is that if we hadn't been left down there like animals that they were treating us like, all of those things would not have happened." Neville reported that her efforts to tell law enforcement officers and the National Guard of her assault were ignored. Neville's prominence and her fortuitous encounter with a member of the Catholic archdiocese in New Orleans during an interview at a local news station meant that her assault received media attention. Others did not.

Obviously, we are not excusing the conduct of the rapists or blaming that conduct on the government. Our point is simply that the overall governmental response in the aftermath of Katrina, shaped as it was by the racial frame of law and order, created conditions of possibility for rape and increased the likelihood that those rapes would be unaddressed. The sexual assaults against women—the vast majority of them black—became markers of black disorder, chaos, and the "animalistic" nature of New Orleans residents; but black women themselves could not occupy the position of victims worthy of rescue. Their injuries were only abstractions that were marshaled to make the larger point about the descent of New Orleans into a literal and figurative black hole. Black women's rape was invoked but not addressed. To borrow from Kimberle Crenshaw, their stories of rape were "voyeuristically included" in a law-and-order campaign.[26] Their specific injury—the fact that they were actually victims—was largely ignored.

The government focused its attention on violence directed against property and violence directed against the rescuers—reports of which have proven to be false or grossly embellished. While these acts of violence could fit comfortably within the frame of law and order, violence against black women's bodies could not. Images of black criminality could work concomitantly with and help to instantiate the law-and-order frame that relies on black disorder; images of black women as innocent victims could do neither. The frames of law and order and black criminality influenced both the exaggeration (overreporting) and the marginalization (underreporting) of violent crimes in ways that make clear that facts don't speak for themselves.

In another example of the law-and-order and black-criminality frames at work in New Orleans, the characterization of the Superdome and the convention center as unsafe facilitated the shift from humanitarian rescue mission to military occupation and security. In part because of the perception of the severe security threat to rescuers, no food, water, or medical care was provided to the convention center until a force of a thousand soldiers and police in full battle gear was sent in to secure the center on September 2 at noon. They were able to do so in twenty minutes and encountered absolutely no resistance, though thousands of people were in the building.

Only one shooting was confirmed in the Superdome, when a soldier shot himself during a scuffle with an attacker. Though New Orleans police chief Eddie Compass reported that he and his officers had retrieved more than thirty weapons from criminals who had been shooting at the rescuers, he later modified his statement to say that this had happened to another unit, a SWAT team at the convention center. The director of the SWAT team, however, reported that his unit had heard gunshots only one time and that his team had recovered no weapons despite aggressive searches.

In retrospect, it is clear that the media both mischaracterized and exaggerated the security threat to the rescue mission. Certainly the chaos in the wake of Katrina and the breakdown of the communications network helped develop a climate in which rumors could and did flourish. Yet under similarly difficult conditions during other natural disasters and even war, reporters have adhered to basic journalistic standards. That they did not under these conditions could be explained as an isolated case of failure under extremely trying circumstances. That might very well be so. Yet, the important part of this story is not that the media failed to observe the basic rules of journalism; it is that the story they told was one people were all too ready to accept. It was a narrative that made sense within the commonly accepted racial frames of law and order and black criminality.

These frames made it difficult for us to make sense of reported instances of "guys who looked like thugs, with pants hanging down around their asses," engaged in frantic efforts to get people collapsing from heat and exhaustion out of the Superdome and into a nearby makeshift medical facility. These images did not make racial sense. There was no ready-made social frame within which the image of black male rescuers could be placed. Existing outside of standard racial frames, black male rescuers present a socially unintelligible image. That we have trouble *seeing* "guys who look like thugs" as rescuers is not a problem of facts. It is a problem of frames. Indeed, the very use of the term "thug" already frames the fact of what they might be doing in a particular way.

CONCLUSION

Lessons from Hurricane Katrina include those about preparedness for natural disasters; coordination among local, state, and federal rescue efforts; and a nation's capacity for empathy and compassion. While it is less than clear that all of these lessons are being learned, we are at least discussing these lessons. Not so with respect to race. As a nation, we rarely talk about race and Katrina anymore. It is almost unspeakable to do so.

Yet, Katrina offers profound insights into how race operates in American society, insights into how various facts about our social life are racially interpreted through frames. As a result of racial frames, black people are both visible (as criminals) and invisible (as victims). Racial frames both capture and displace us—discursively and materially. More than shaping whether we see black people as criminal or innocent, perpetrator or victim, these frames shape whether we see black people at all. Indeed, one might reasonably ask: Where have all the black people gone, long time passing? It is not hyperbolic to say that post-Katrina black New Orleanians have become a part of an emerging social category: the disappeared. A critical lesson of Katrina is that civil rights advocacy groups need to think harder about frames, particular when making interventions into natural disasters involving African Americans.

As Michele Landis Dauber reminds us, the template for the American social welfare system has been disaster relief, and the extent to which people are entitled to any form of government resources has always depended upon the claimants' ability to "nar-rat[e] their deprivation as a disaster—a sudden loss for which the claimant is not responsible."[27] In the case of Katrina, this disaster-relief conception of welfare would seem to promote an immediate national response to aid the hurricane victims. The problem for black people and for other nonwhites, however, as Dauber herself notes, is that racial minorities' claims to victim status have always been fraught "because they are highly likely to be cast as a 'disaster' for the dominant racial group.[28] Implicit in Dauber's analysis is the idea that the move to realign America's racial discourse and policy away from its current distortions must confront the complex problem of racial frames. The existence of racial frames makes it enormously difficult to incorporate "just the facts" into an argu-ment about racism. Those facts will rarely, if ever, be able to escape completely the interpretational reach and normative appeal of racial frames about color blindness and black cultural dysfunc-tionality.

What is required is likely to be more in the nature of a social movement than a social survey. Facts will always play a crucial role, but just as the successes of the civil rights movement were born of organized struggle, so too must our efforts to shift racial frames ground themselves in a broader and more organic orientation than raw empiricism. People came to see the facts of de jure segre-gation differently not because new facts emerged about its harms but because new interpretations of those facts were made possible by social organization on the ground that pushed the courts to-ward a new consensus. We believe the same is true today.

NOTES

This chapter draws from and builds upon Cheryl I. Harris, "White Washing Race; Scapegoating Culture," *California Law Review* (2006) (forthcoming) (book review).

1. Cited in Aaron Kinney, " 'Looting' or 'Finding'?" *Salon,* September 1, 2005.

2. www.snopes.com/Katrina/photos/looters.asp.

3. Cited in Kinney, " 'Looting' or 'Finding'?"

4. Ibid.

5. One study of local television news stories on crime and public opinion illustrates the strong association between criminal behavior and racial identity. Participants were shown an identical news story under three different conditions: one group witnessed a version in which the perpetrator was white; another group saw a version in which the perpetrator was black; and a third group viewed a version in which there was no picture of the perpetrator. Following the screening, the participants in the first, white-perpetrator group were less likely to recall having seen a suspect than subjects in the second, black-perpetrator group. Among those in the third group, who saw no image of the perpetrator, over 60 percent erroneously recalled seeing a perpetrator, and in 70 percent of those cases viewers identified that nonexistent image as black. See Franklin Gilliam Jr. and Shanto Iyengar, "Prime Suspects: The Influence of Local Television News on the Viewing Public," *American Journal of Political Science* 44 (2000):560.

6. Roger Schank, "Tell Me a Story," *Narrative and Intelligence* 71 (1995).

7. A more nuanced formulation suggests, "Like well-accepted theories that guide our interpretation of data, schemas incline us to interpret data consistent with our biases." See Jerry Kang, "Trojan Horses of Races," *Harvard Law Review* 118 (2005):1489, 1515.

8. We do not intend to ignore the tremendous loss suffered in the Gulf region more broadly: we focus on New Orleans because of its unique

position in the national imagination, as well as its pre-Katrina racial demographics. Indeed, New Orleans was not just a city that had come to be predominantly black; it was a city that was culturally marked as black. As one noted historian has stated, "The unique culture of south Louisiana derives from black Creole culture." Quoted in "Buffetted by Katrina, City's Complex Black Community Struggles to Regroup," Associated Press, October 4, 2005, www.msnbc.com.

9. Or fend for themselves and be punished for it. A particularly harrowing account of official indifference and hostility comes from the ordeal of two emergency room workers who had the misfortune of being in New Orleans for a conference when Hurricane Katrina struck. After their hotel in the French Quarter closed, they, along with several hundred others, collected money to hire buses for their evacuation, but the buses were prevented from entering the city. When the workers attempted to flee on foot, they were directed to wait on the interstate for rescue that never came. Neither the police nor the National Guard provided them with food or water. When the group managed to find food for themselves and set up a makeshift camp, they were repeatedly dispersed at gunpoint by the police. When they attempted to walk across the bridge into the neighboring city of Gretna, they were again turned back at gunpoint by Gretna police. See Larry Bradshaw and Lorrie Beth Slonsky, "Trapped in New Orleans," September 6, 2005, www.counterpunch.org/bradshaw0906 2005.html.

10. On a nationally broadcast telethon to raise money for the victims of Katrina, Kanye West departed from the scripted remarks to say, "I hate the way they portray us in the media. You see a black family: it says they are looting. You see a white family; it says they have been looking for food. And you know, it has been five days, because most of the people are black, and even for me to complain about it, I would be a hypocrite, because I have tried to turn away from the TV because it is too hard to watch. So now I am calling my business manager right now to

see what is the biggest amount I can give. And just imagine if I was down there and those are my people down there." Commenting on the slow pace of the government's response, he said, "George Bush doesn't care about black people." NBC immediately cut to another star on the program and censored West's remarks from the West Coast feed of the program. It also issued the following disclaimer: "Kanye West departed from the scripted comments that were prepared for him, and his opinions in no way represent the views of the networks. It would be most unfortunate if the efforts of the artists who participated tonight and the generosity of millions of Americans who are helping those in need are overshadowed by one person's opinion." "Rapper Kanye West Accuses Bush of Racism; NBC Apologizes," *CBC Arts*, September 3, 2005, www.cbc.ca/story/arts/national/2005/09/03/ Arts/kanye_west_katrina20050903.html.

11. This was Howard Dean's view. In an address to the National Baptist Convention he stated, "As survivors are evacuated, order is restored, the water slowly begins to recede, and we sort through the rubble, we must also begin to come to terms with the ugly truth that skin color, age and economics played a deadly role in who survived and who did not." "Excerpts of DNC Chairman Howard Dean's Remarks to the National Baptist Convention of America, Inc.," U.S. Newswire, September 8, 2005, www.usnewswire.com/

12. While some have argued that class was a more salient factor than race in explaining who was affected, we do not think that given the country's history of de jure and de facto racial subordination, race can be so neatly disaggregated from class. Particularly in the context of New Orleans—a city that was predominantly black and predominantly poor—the fact that those left on the overpasses and in the Superdome were black had everything to do with why they were poor. The point is not to reproduce another unhelpful version of the race-versus-class debate but to avoid sublimating the racial dimension of the issues raised by Katrina. Recent survey analysis suggests that race

was in fact a crucial factor in explaining who was in harm's way. See "Katrina Hurts Blacks and Poor Victims Most," CNN/*USA Today*/Gallup Poll, October 25, 2005.

13. Both the Reverend Jesse Jackson and Representative Cynthia McKinney drew a link between the events in the Gulf and slavery. In response to a question by Anderson Cooper on CNN about whether race was a determinative factor in the federal government's response to Katrina, Jackson replied, "It is at least a factor. Today I saw 5,000 African Americans on the I-10 causeway desperate, perishing, dehydrated, babies dying. It looked like Africans in the hull of a slave ship. It was so ugly and so obvious. Have we missed this catastrophe because of indifference and ineptitude or is it a combination of both? And certainly I think the issue of race as a factor will not go away from this equation." Jesse Jackson, Remarks on *360 Degrees*, CNN, September 2, 2005. In an address on the floor of the House of Representatives on September 8, 2005, Representative McKinney said, "As I saw the African Americans, mostly African-American families ripped apart, I could only think about slavery, families ripped apart, herded into what looked like concentration camps." Cynthia McKinney, "Text of Remarks Delivered on the Floor of the House on Sept. 8, 2005," reprinted in "A Few Thoughts on the State of Our Nation," September 12, 2005, www.counterpunch.org/mckinney09122005.html.

14. "Huge Racial Divide over Katrina and Its Consequences," Report of the Pew Research Center for People and the Press, September 8, 2005, 2; available at http://people-press.org/reports/display.php3?ReportID=255.

15. As Gary Blasi contends, "If we store social categories in our heads by means of prototypes or exemplars rather than statistics, then our basic cognitive mechanisms not only predispose us toward stereotypes . . . , but also limit the potentially curative effect of information that contradicts the statistical assumptions about base rates that are embedded in our stereotypes." Gary Blasi, "Advocacy Against the Stereotype," *UCLA Law Review* 49 (2002):1241, 1256–57.

16. See Lee Cokorinos, *The Assault on Diversity* (Institute for Democracy Studies, 2002), tracing the network of conservative activists and organizations that have waged a well-funded campaign over two decades to change the corpus of civil rights laws, end affirmative action, and reframe the political discourse on race and racism.

17. This should not suggest that she was without any compassion. She went on to say, "[The bodies] have to go somewhere. These are people's families. They have to—they still have to have dignity." It's precisely our point that one can have compassion and still see black people through racial frames. *Paula Zahn Now*, CNN, September 8, 2005.

18. See Michael Ignatieff, "The Broken Contract," *New York Times*, September 25, 2005 (reporting that a woman held at the convention center asserted, "We are American" during a TV interview, demonstrating both anger and astonishment that she would have to remind Americans of that fact and that the social contract had failed).

19. Note that this frame is simultaneously inclusionary and exclusionary. To the extent that it asserts black citizenship, it seeks to include black people within the nation-state. However, it excludes noncitizens, black as well as others, from the circle of care based on lack of formal American belonging. This is deeply problematic but it reveals the limited space within which blacks could assert legitimate claims on national empathy.

20. See Anna Johnson, "Jackson Lashes Out at Bush over Hurricane Response, Criticizes Media for Katrina Coverage," AP Alert, September 3, 2005 (reporting that the Red Cross asserted that it could not enter New Orleans on orders from the National Guard and local authorities). A principal reason for the delay was that government officials believed that they had to prepare a complicated military operation rather than a relief effort. See "Misinformation Seen Key in Katrina Delays," UPI Top Stories, September 30, 2005.

21. See Brian Thevenot and Gordon Russell, "Reports of Anarchy at the Superdome Overstated," *Seattle Times*, September 26, 2005 (reporting

that "the vast majority of reported atrocities committed by evacuees have turned out to be false, or at least unsupported by any evidence, according to key military, law enforcement, medical and civilian officers in a position to know." See also Andrew Gumbel, "After the Storm, US Media Held to Account for Exaggerated Tales of Katrina Chaos," *Los Angeles Times,* September 28, 2005.

22. Susannah Rosenblatt and James Rainey, "Reports of Post-Katrina Mayhem May Have Been Overblown," *Los Angeles Times,* September 27, 2005.

23. Thevenot and Russell, "Reports of Anarchy."

24. See "40 Rapes Reported in Hurricane Katrina, Rita Aftermath," NewOrleansChannel.com, wsdu, http://msnbc.msn.com/id/1059 0305; Nancy Cook Lauer, "Rape-Reporting Procedure Missing After Hurricane," Women's eNews, www.womensenews.org/article.cfm/ dyn/aid/2448.

25. See Charmaine Neville, "How We Survived the Flood," transcript of interview given to New Orleans media outlets, September 5, 2005, www.counterpunch.org/neville09072005.html.

26. Kimberle Crenshaw, "Mapping the Margins: Intersectionality, Identity Politics, and Violence Against Women of Color," *Stanford Law Review* 43 (1991):1241, 1261.

27. Michele Landis Dauber, "Fate, Responsibility, and 'Natural' Disaster Relief: Narrating the American Welfare State," *Law and Society* 33 (1999):257, 264.

28. Ibid., 307.

8

WHILE VISIONS OF DEVIANCE DANCED IN THEIR HEADS
Katheryn Russell-Brown

Who are you gonna believe, me or your lying eyes?

For centuries American criminal law penalized Black skin. The sanctions took many forms: the slave codes, Black Laws, Black Codes, and segregation-era statutes. With stunning consistency, American law placed a criminal marker on black folks' doings and goings on. Make no mistake, it was dark skin itself that was being punished. The slave codes made it illegal for enslaved blacks to gather in groups (unless someone white was present), walk about without written permission from their masters, or engage in religious worship, to name a few. The slave noose was drawn so tight that it could not be shed simply by stepping onto free soil.[1] Black skin equaled slave skin—unless you could prove otherwise.

The Black Codes and the oxymoronic separate-but-equal laws were the next legal iteration of blacks as other, as deviant. Following the abolition of slavery, blacks were no longer chattel. However, they still were not free from white domination. The taint of black skin, as proclaimed by the law, persisted and reared its Hydra head in every social, political, legal, and economic arena. The law took great pains to make sure that blacks were never entitled to the same treatment as whites. The fact that there were laws that made it illegal to put black and white criminals on the same chain gang dramatically illustrates this point.

Could enslaved Africans-cum-blacks, and their allies, do anything about any of this? As one of my perplexed white students asked in class, "Did slaves have *any* means of redress?" Well, no. There was no legal redress, no slavery ombudsman.[2]

Today we still have a race-infected criminal justice system. By any measure (e.g., arrests, prosecutorial charges, convictions, and sentencing), at the bar of justice blacks do not fare as well as whites. Not close. While the obvious bars of legalized racial injustice have been removed, other egregious and insidious forms have taken shape. I label this the difference between racial injustice and racial "*a*justice." Racial "injustice" refers to a system that operates in a racially biased manner, one that disfavors people of color, a system that does not work properly—the system we currently have. Racial "ajustice," on the other hand, describes the failure of the law to operate as a way to mete out justice. Here the law fails not because of what it does but because of what it does not do. Thus, racial ajustice describes a structural process that acts to disenfranchise the poor and those of color. Something must be done to ensure that the law is applied to punish evident harms against marginalized groups.

Which brings me to hurricane Katrina.

If asked about the crimes that occurred during and after Katrina, most folks would probably mention looting, rape, shootings at police aircraft, and other "street" crimes that received broad media coverage. We soon learned that many of the reports of crime were grossly overstated—many have now been dismissed as urban legends. Further, the crimes most of us visualize as associated with Katrina involve young black men, either acting in concert or individually running amok. But if we look at Katrina and the only crimes we see are looting and rape, then we miss a much larger story of crime and justice.

IMAGINING CRIME

These racialized images are consistent with our perceptions of what constitutes crime and who commits crime. The majority of Americans envision street crime when they think about crime. For most of us, when we "see" crime, it involves an offense committed by individuals against other individuals. Crime is when one man hits another over the head and steals his wallet; when someone's car is stolen; when a woman is raped at gunpoint; when a child is kidnapped from her bedroom; when someone pickpockets another's wallet; or when a man dies after being hit over the head while walking down the street.

The corollary proposition that goes hand in hand with this stock and narrow view of crime is the race-based perception that most Americans have of who the real criminals are. Most of us, regardless of race and gender, fear young black men. Even though most crime involves offenders and victims of the same race, we steadfastly believe that our greatest crime threat is at the hands of a young black man. When we put these two beliefs together—that crime is defined as street crime and that young black men are criminals—what we have is a collective, acute, national fear of black men engaging in acts of violence. Further, these propositions ensure that black men remain in the bull's-eye of the justice system. In fact, if the system is working properly, its net must capture primarily black men. However, we can step out of this confining box and consider an alternative way to examining crime, criminals, and justice.

REDEFINING CRIME

"Crime" is generally defined as an act (or failure to act) that violates local, state, federal, or international law. Applying this definition to Katrina provides us with a fresh opportunity to reconsider how we "see" crime and justice. We can look at some Katrina-related events that could be deemed unlawful, possibly criminal, certainly wrong:

- Denial of access, by law enforcement officials, to hundreds of fleeing New Orleans residents who sought entry onto a public bridge (hate crime, §1983 Civil Rights Act violation, and false imprisonment)
- Delay in the search and rescue efforts for hurricane victims (negligence, wrongful death)
- Inadequate police, fire, and rescue efforts on behalf of hurricane victims (negligence, wrongful death)
- Failure to construct an adequate levee system able to withstand a category 4 hurricane in a city that, according to all indicators, would face a deadly hurricane (negligence, wrongful death)
- Absence of a feasible evacuation plan for New Orleans, a city in which a large number of the residents, who lived in areas projected to face the most damage, did not have the means to evacuate (wrongful death, negligence)
- Inadequate federal strategy and funding for handling millions of displaced hurricane residents (negligence, intentional infliction of emotional distress, and negligent infliction of emotional distress)

- Inadequate funding for locating the lost and the dead, resulting in public desecration of the deceased (loss of consortium, negligent infliction of emotional distress)
- Adoption of a New Orleans rebuilding plan that allows for substantial rebuilding in most areas except the Lower Ninth Ward (negligence, unlawful taking)
- Refusal by the White House to release requested Katrina-related papers for investigation by a Senate panel (obstruction of justice)[3]

This short list is revealing. At every turn, official responses to the hurricane worked against the interests of poor blacks. There was insufficient advance planning, a bumbling local-state-federal response to the impending hurricane (including a failed evacuation effort), and woefully inadequate resources to handle the injured, the stranded, the lost, and the dead. Although some of the state and private actions that caused wide-scale harm cannot be prosecuted (e.g., because of legal immunity), many of the wrongs are actionable. A more detailed look at a few of these incidents underscores the need to "see" Katrina's crimes and punish them.

The Gretna showdown ranks high on the long list of Katrina's parade of horribles.[4] Hundreds of people, mostly black, who sought to flee the rising floodwaters in New Orleans were blocked from walking across a public bridge. Police officers from three different jurisdictions stood guard and prevented would-be evacuees from escaping through Gretna's mostly white suburban bedroom community. Gretna's sheriff stated that he did not want his town to become another New Orleans.

There were reports that the police officers guarding the bridge had their firearms aimed at approaching evacuees, reports that the police fired shots into the air to scare people away, and reports that whites were permitted to cross the police barriers and escape to safety. Federal law recognizes that law enforcement officers, acting under the color of law, are prohibited from discriminating on the basis of race.[5] Surely the harms associated with the Gretna standoff are ones that the law seeks to remedy. At least one politician, Georgia congressperson Cynthia McKinney, has called for an investigation into the incident to determine whether the racially disparate responses by law enforcement officers are classifiable as hate crimes.

The Gretna standoff epitomizes posthurricane travesties. The government's failure to prepare epitomizes pre-Katrina travesties. Long before Katrina's landfall, it was predicted that a New Orleans hurricane could result in one of the nation's deadliest natural disasters. In fact, it led the list of the top three predicted natural disasters. In 2004, FEMA conducted a New Orleans hurricane simulation—"Hurricane Pam"—to assess how to respond to a Katrina-like disaster. It was determined that the city needed to adopt a method for evacuating the city's poorest residents, those living closest to outdated levees, those living below sea level, and those least likely to have access to a car.[6] We should look to the law for redress here, for the state's failure to heed the warnings and the foreseeable deaths and massive destruction that followed.

Plans to rebuild New Orleans surfaced quickly following Katrina. Less than six months passed before the mayor, in conjunction with a city planning firm, unveiled a detailed plan for a new New Orleans. The project outlined major development and rebuilding in virtually all of New Orleans, except the Lower Ninth Ward, where 98 percent of the fourteen thousand residents are black.

At the same time that New Orleans was making plans to build the first twenty-first-century city, there were hundreds of not-yet-identified dead bodies in makeshift morgues across the state; thousands of displaced residents scattered across the country; thousands of displaced residents who were trying to return to New Orleans; and children and family members who were still missing. To paraphrase one New Orleans woman who lost her home in the flood and five months later was still looking for her elderly mother, "Where are the government's priorities? There's a bunch of talk about rebuilding New Orleans. Some of us are still trying to locate our family members." The law should be used to redress these wrongs, whether they were the result of intentional harm or negligence.

For some harms, there is no redress. The Lower Ninth Ward's neighborhoods represented generations of families with tight kinship bonds. This made Katrina's devastation that much greater because "home" for the black poor in New Orleans was not the larger city of New Orleans but a small grid of streets. Home has a much different meaning for the middle class—they are more likely to leave the hometowns they were raised in, more likely to have more than one home, and more likely to be "at home in the world." For New Orleans's poorest residents, there was no place to evacuate to and no way to get there. For the poor who were fortunate enough to escape safely, returning to rebuild poses severe, perhaps insurmountable challenges.

There are laws on the books that can be used to prosecute those responsible for many of Katrina's harms. Whether such legal actions would be successful is not what's most important; what is imperative is that some attempt be made to have legal *acknowledgment* of the multitude of harms, physical and emotional, wrought by state officials in the wake of Katrina.

The effort to identify those liable for Katrina's harms is more than just symbolic. Prosecutions targeting those responsible for the poor planning and execution of disaster relief would send a clear message that the wide-scale offenses committed against Katrina victims, mostly black and poor, did not escape notice—the victims did not "disappear." The failure to recognize an offense because of the victim's race and class status is symptomatic of racial ajustice—a system that has selective vision when it comes to what constitutes crime and harm.

The failure to use or attempt to use the law to punish obvious, egregious, and large-scale offenses also makes it likely that blacks will become even more distrustful of the government in general and the criminal justice system in particular. One commentator observed, "Something about Katrina is making [black] people remember their own personal injustices."[7] Most blacks believe that the government would have acted sooner and done substantially more if the victims had been white.[8] Whites saw something different. Most believed that race had no effect on the government's recovery efforts.

This racial divide reflects deep-seated suspicious about the government, its response, and ultimately its racial agenda. For example, many blacks believe that the government will prevent most black New Orleanians from returning to their homes, that it plans to make New Orleans a white city. These conspiracy theories are further fueled by studies indicating that *80 percent* of New Orleans's black population will not be able to return to the city unless more state and federal aid is made available.[9]

AJUSTICE AFOOT

The above (nonexhaustive) list of Katrina's wrongs offers another way of interpreting the events surrounding the storm. The fact that these incidents are not widely characterized as offenses—criminal or civil wrongs—indicates there is a void in the public's perception of what constitutes harm. This is racial ajustice at work. Catastrophic harms against marginalized groups go unnamed and unpunished—the law does not operate. Patent wrongs are not pursued by the state.

This happens because there is no space for these offenses within the mainstream media narrative on race, crime, and justice. These wrongs do not fit with our stereotypical, race-based images of offenders and offending. We should be as concerned about the absence of law as we are about unjust legal outcomes. The absence of law echoes an earlier historical period when harms visited upon blacks—physical brutality, rape, and the denial of civil liberties and civil rights—were not recognized as legal wrongs.

These harms are hard to see and difficult to characterize as crime because we face overpowering racialized images of who embodies criminality and what the criminal threat is. Throughout the media, in varying degrees, images linking blackness with deviance are on display. On television these images are everywhere—in music videos, the nightly news, reality TV programs, daytime television talk shows, cartoons, and commercials. Black men provide a familiar resting place for deviance in the American mind: the *criminalblackman*.[10] This rampant image makes it easy to believe that black people are always looters, never finders. But in this case there is no readily identifiable black man to point the finger at.

Another reason these harms have been overlooked is that they do not fit into easy, media-digestible pieces. They are detailed, complicated, and not easily captured in sound bites. They are a far cry from the typical crime fare to which we have become accustomed. But while we must not ignore street crimes, if we are to take crime seriously, we cannot adopt narrow, big-business-serving definitions of what constitutes harm. We must reconsider and broaden our view of how crime is defined.

VISUALIZING JUSTICE

The spectacle of Katrina is powerful and compelling in part because there are so few opportunities to openly discuss the workings of race and class at the national level. The rarity of these events may help to explain why the discussions they generate tend not to break new ground. We engage in a routine pattern of responses and counterresponses as these cases—e.g., the O.J. Simpson criminal trial, the LAPD/Rodney King case, and Katrina—play themselves out on the big stage. These responses include arguing about whether race affected the outcome of events; hand-wringing over polls that show a racial divide between blacks and whites; discussing the extent to which there has been racial progress in the country; and predicting whether we are likely to repeat the same mistakes the next time around. By the time this exhausting and contentious process has run its course, there is little energy or will to dig further and ask what justice means and how we would know it if we saw it. It is this extra digging, however, that provides us with the possibility for real change, for transformative justice.

Understanding Katrina requires that we take an expanded view of crime so that we can determine whether there has been "justice." We should treat "justice" as a verb—a goal that requires continuous action, not a state we achieve. Frederick Douglass's admonition to "agitate, agitate, agitate" is well applied here.

In broadening our perspective on crime, we can see that the real crimes of Katrina went unnamed and unchecked. These harms highlight the sociostructural aspects of racial rights and racial relief. The short list of some of Katrina's more egregious harms demonstrates how city planning, urban renewal, law enforcement, and local, state, and national politics intersected to effectively deny black citizens fair and equitable treatment.

Katrina's harms are multitudinous and broad. In order for these offenses to be treated as crimes, we have to reimagine what justice means. In the long run, the failure to engage a broader vision of justice leaves in place a one-dimensional and static view of what constitutes harm in our society, and this limits the ways in which these harms can be redressed. Have we accepted a justice system that focuses almost exclusively on street crime? In this fog, other wrongs involving serious harms routinely go unnoticed and unpunished.

The cavalry did not arrive in time. Katrina offers little in terms of an optimistic vision of equality and understanding between the races. It does, however, offer hope in the form of an object lesson. It compels us to continue to question the dominant narrative on race and crime. It exhorts us to adopt new meanings and expectations for crime and justice. Ultimately Katrina commands us to believe our lying eyes and to do something about what we see.

NOTES

1. *Dred Scott v. Sandford,* 60 U.S. 393 (1857).
2. A term coined by my colleague, Melissa Bamba, to describe what such an officer of redress might have been titled.
3. Commentators have identified other Katrina-related offenses.

See, e.g., Mike Davis and Anthony Fontenot, "25 Questions About the Murder of New Orleans," *The Nation*, September 30, 2005, www.thenation.com/doc/20051017/davis; Glen Ford and Peter Gamble, "Fighting the Theft of New Orleans: The Rhythm of Resistance," www.blackcommentator.com, January 19, 2006 (issue 167).

4. See, e.g., Gardiner Harris, "Police in Suburbs Blocked Evacuees, Witnesses Report," *New York Times*, September 10, 2005. For a series of radio interviews with Katrina victims (some of whom attempted to cross the bridge and escape through Gretna) see "After the Flood," *This American Life* (296), NPR, September 9–11, 2005. Transcript available online.

5. In December 2005, a class-action lawsuit was filed in the U.S. District Court for the Eastern District of Louisiana. The lawsuit states that the plaintiffs were turned away by police and prohibited from walking over the Westbank Expressway into Gretna. The suit alleges that Gretna officials violated their constitutional rights and their civil rights. *Tracy Dickerson, et. al. v. City of Gretna, et. al.*, Case 2:05-cv=06667-MVL-ALC.

6. Alan Berube and Steven Raphael, "Access to Cars in New Orleans," www.brookings.edu/metro/20050915_katrinacarstables.pdf.

7. "Blacks Rally Around Katrina Cause," CBS News, September 9, 2005, www.cbsnews.com/stories/2005/09/09/katrina/printable829498.shtml.

8. See, generally, Pew Research Center, "Two-in-Three Critical of Bush's Relief Efforts," September 8, 2005, http://people-press.org/reports; Susan Page and Mari Puente, "Poll Shows Racial Divide on Storm Response," *USA Today*, September 12, 2005, www.usatoday.com; "Poll: Bush Approval Drops," ABC News, September 12, 2005. (analysis by Gary Langer), www.abcnews.go.com/Politics/print?id=1117357; "Reaction to Katrina Split on Racial Lines," *CNN.com*, September 13, 2005, www.cnn.com; and Glen Ford and Peter Gamble,

"Katrina: A Study," www.blackcommentator.com, January 5, 2006, (Issue 165).

9. See, e.g., James Dao, "Study Says 80% of New Orleans Blacks May Not Return," *New York Times,* January 27, 2006.

10. Katheryn K. Russell *The Color of Crime* (New York: New York University Press, 1998), 3.

Part Five

RIGHTS AND SHARED HUMANITIES

FROM WRONGS TO RIGHTS: HURRICANE KATRINA FROM A GLOBAL PERSPECTIVE
Adrien Katherine Wing

I have a love-hate relationship with Louisiana. I have enjoyed the legendary hospitality I have received when I lectured at the predominantly white Louisiana State University and the predominantly black Southern University law schools, both in Baton Rouge, the state capital. I have loved eating sugary beignets and drinking café au lait at the world famous Café du Monde restaurant in the New Orleans French Quarter. I have listened joyfully to jazz in Preservation Hall and attended the Essence Music Festival in the Superdome alongside the late Johnnie Cochran. I have gorged on tasty specialties like shrimp po boys and drunk daiquiris legally while walking down the street. I have danced at the Mayor's Ball during Mardi Gras when my law school friend Marc Morial was the Big Easy's mayor. For a few summers during the 1990s, I also supervised a New Orleans version of the Amer-I-Can youth program owned by football Hall of Famer and actor Jim Brown. I have even won money gambling at Harrah's on the waterfront. New Orleans has been my good luck charm.

And then there is the dark side. I have driven through rural areas that resembled the antebellum South—big beautiful plantations and little broken-down shacks. I have spoken with Chocolate City teenagers who could barely write their names because of a failed school system abandoned by anyone with money. I have sat in a juvenile court and watched a parade of dark-skinned black boys head off to jail—not a white or high-yellow-skinned black among them. I have visited the Desire projects, which were far from desirable.

And even though I felt sorry for the people of New Orleans after Hurricane Katrina, there was one place that I hoped was flooded by the hurricane. It was my great-great-grandfather's house. Why would I want my ancestor's house to be flooded? Why would I wish that on anyone's home? My ancestor was Confederate general Pierre Gustave Toutant Beauregard, who fired on Fort Sumter, starting the Civil War. He lived in New Orleans at 1113 Chartres Street after the war, from 1865 to 1867. An engineer by training, he was the president of the New Orleans, Jackson, and Great Northern Railroad at the time. He was a glorious war hero to the southerners even though their side and their cause had lost.

Because of Beauregard's heroic status, this home that he merely rented was restored to its antebellum glory in the twentieth century, and it is now a tourist attraction known as the Beauregard-Keyes House. The house was built in 1826 for the wealthy auctioneer Joseph Le Carpentier; its other famous occupant was Mrs. Frances Parkinson Keyes, a novelist who lived in it from 1944 to 1970. Our Pruitt family lore indicates that the general's picture graced a place of prominence in my maternal grandmother Katherine's house, even though she never knew him personally.

When I made my first trip to New Orleans, my mom's family encouraged me to visit this house. "You've got to see it!" they said. I will never forget the guide dressed in a splendid antebellum gown, who showed the small group of tourists the very dignified portraits of the general and his lovely family. I will also never forget the guide's face when I told the group that those women on the wall were not the general's only family. He had black descendants as well, and I was one of them. She blanched and said that she knew that the general was like the other southern gentlemen of his time, but she was not allowed to talk about that. Then she hurried us on to look at the cookbooks.

I was dismissed. My family's claim was dismissed. I mused that miscegenation between white war heroes and black slaves or servants was not a proper topic for a tour as we walked into the bedroom containing an actual bed of the general's. Did my great-great-grandmother Sally Hardin sleep in that bed? Or did she sleep in the former slave quarters in the back? The guide said that twenty slaves/servants had lived in the slave quarters at one point to take care of the needs of the few whites living in the main house. Was my great-grandmother Susan Beauregard conceived in that very bed, or in the slave quarters that later became a stable, and then a garage, and eventually a study for Mrs. Keyes?

I had always hated the fact that through my veins coursed the blood of a general who fought to preserve a way of life that had enslaved my ancestors. So in September 2005, I hoped that his house was buried deep beneath the floodwaters—tourist attraction no more. But the house was located in the French Quarter—the high ground. Additionally, the house itself was raised—a wonderful example of the home style where twin curving staircases in the front permitted guests to walk up to the front door with its wide porch. This house was spared, while the modern-day descendants of so many slaves who lived on the low ground lost everything.

Although I hate that the general and I are linked through time,

there is one part of his legacy that I have accepted. His family orig-
inally came from France, and my family, the black descendants,
have always learned French. My study of French turned into a career as an international lawyer and, now, a law professor. I also direct my law school's summer program in Arcachon, France.

So when I saw dark-skinned black people wading through
floodwaters after Hurricane Katrina, I looked at the tragedy with
the eyes of an international lawyer. I had to double check to see if I
was watching the CNN International channel instead of the CNN
National News. The on-air presence of CNN International corre-
spondents Jeff Koinange and Christiane Amanpour reinforced this
notion. Were we in the Congo? No, Koinange was broadcasting live
from Bourbon Street. The world could see what I had long known.
Behind the New Orleans that I loved and hated, there was the third
world hidden in plain sight within the first world.

This Essay will bring an international lens to bear on Hurricane
Katrina. I will first adress how the U.S. government's stupendous
mishandling of the disaster made us appear to those living in other
countries. Then, I will discuss international law and its possible
application to the Hurricane Katrina situation. In all the incessant
media coverage about the hurricane and its aftermath, I am aware
of no story that looked at the international law aspect of the
tragedy.

HOW THE UNITED STATES LOOKED
TO THE REST OF THE WORLD

Katrina was called a "black storm" in the European media. Some in
the African media expressed shock, while others thought the situation was to be expected, given how poorly black people have been
treated in the United States for more than two hundred years. The

hurricane stripped away the veneer of equality and color blindness and showed the whole world that the superpower, or "hyperpower" as the French call us, still had a race problem. Dr. Arjun Sengupta, United Nations Human Rights Commission special reporter on extreme poverty, visited New Orleans and Baton Rouge in late October and called the conditions "shocking and gross violations of human rights."

The army troops called in to patrol New Orleans symbolized the failure of domestic law and order. "Anarchy in the USA," screamed a headline in a British paper. "Apocalypse Now" asserted a German source. The irony was that four thousand members of the Louisiana National Guard, which normally would have been the first national responders, were bogged down in Iraq, rather than at home when disaster struck. The French newspaper *Le Monde* queried, "Is it well advised to spend hundreds of millions—make it billions—of dollars to make war in Iraq when America is incapable of protecting its own citizens?" The same paper asked, "Why did the Bush administration fail in its first great security test since the September 11, 2001, attacks?" The Spanish paper *El Vanguardia* stated, "Katrina has highlighted the worst and most unjust [aspects] of the U.S. . . . . a superpower in decline."

The military man in charge, Lieutenant General Russel Honore, a native of New Orleans, had to remind his troops that they were not in Baghdad. They should not point their weapons at civilians. These people were not aliens to Honore—they were home folks. Ironically, the general's own son was in Iraq too.

The army was not enough. Certain rich people hired special Israeli security experts to protect their properties. Some security people who usually work in Iraq as private contractors, i.e., mercenaries, said they preferred working in Iraq to New Orleans.

One of my friends thought that General Honore was white,

until I explained that he was a classic high-yellow black Creole, like my own ancestors. These descendants of mixtures between blacks and whites dating back to slave days were once called mulattoes, quadroons, or octoroons, depending on their degree of whiteness. The Creoles still disproportionately account for the black elites of Louisiana. All the black mayors of New Orleans—current mayor Ray Nagin, and former mayors Marc Morial, Ernest Morial, and Sidney Barthelemy—have been part of this sector of blacks. You did not see them wading through the floodwaters or stranded at the Superdome. They drove out. The race problem was not just black and white, but also within the historically color-conscious black community as well.

The world could see the tragedy unfolding in the aftermath of Hurricane Katrina and responded as it would to any third-world crisis. More than a hundred countries contributed money, including $25,000 from poor Sri Lanka, still recovering from the December 2004 tsunami. (Sadly, the United States did not reciprocate proportionally to the relief efforts in Pakistan soon after an earthquake that may have killed more than one hundred thousand people.) A Mexican army convoy arrived, marking the first time the Mexican military had operated north of the Rio Grande since Texas won its independence in 1846. Cuba offered more than money as well—1,600 disaster-trained doctors and eighty-three tons of medicine. This generous offer was made despite the forty-five-year U.S. embargo against the Communist island nation. Antiquated U.S. policies dictated that we could not accept this offer from our enemy. Ironically, almost no one dies when monster hurricanes strike Cuba, because of the country's well thought-out and executed national evacuation plans. In our monumental hubris, we think that we have nothing to learn from Cuba.

The U.S. handling of the Katrina disaster did not help our

global image, and the implications may be felt for many years to come. Coupled with our mishandling of the Iraq situation, Katrina may indeed signal to our enemies, like al Qaeda, that the superpower is weakening. I pray that no one decides to destroy a dam or destabilize a levee system in some other city. Would our response be any better today?

INTERNATIONAL LAW AND
ITS APPLICABILITY TO HURRICANE KATRINA

Although I will primarily emphasize a little-known nonbinding international document called the Guiding Principles on Internal Displacement ("Guiding Principles"),[1] I will first discuss some binding and nonbinding treaties, as well as the distinction between refugees and internally displaced persons.

Two international treaties that the United States is obligated to enforce have direct relevance to the Katrina situation: the International Convention on Civil and Political Rights (ICCPR) and the International Convention on the Elimination of Race Discrimination (ICERD).[2] These treaties are binding on the United States because the president signed them, and then the Senate ratified them. They contain a variety of obligations such as rights to nondiscrimination; equal protection under the law; life; human dignity; recognition as a person; security of the person; electoral rights; right to participate in governance; and freedom of movement. These obligations mandate the United States to offer human rights protections to those persons displaced in the aftermath of Hurricane Katrina. Undoubtedly, international law scholars will write detailed analyses concerning possible U.S. violations of these treaties.

There are other international treaties that could be applicable to a Katrina-type tragedy one day, but they are not binding on the United States now. While the president signed them, the Senate has not ratified them yet. These include the International Convention on Economic, Social and Cultural Rights (ICESCR), the Convention on Rights of the Child (CRC), and the International Convention on the Elimination of Discrimination Against Women (CEDAW).[3] Even though these agreements are not yet binding on the United States, as a signatory, we are still required not to do anything that would defeat the object and purpose of these treaties. This is unfortunately not equivalent to having an active obligation to implement them.[4]

In addition to the above-mentioned documents, there are other agreements that might apply depending on how we define the people affected by Hurricane Katrina. Some commentators called the victims "refugees." After all, they really did resemble the poor, homeless, and hungry unfortunates in such places as the Sudan. Nonetheless, because the evacuees did not flee outside their national boundaries, they are technically called "internally displaced persons" under international law. The proper designation is important, since it has implications for what laws might apply. For example, refugees are protected by the 1951 Convention Relating to the Status of Refugees, whereas internally displaced person are not.[5]

Under the aegis of Sudanese diplomat Francis Deng, the United Nations developed the Guiding Principles in 1998, since the existing international treaties mentioned above all contained gaps in coverage, especially for internally displaced persons. The effort was undertaken in part because of the more than fifty million people worldwide who have been internally uprooted by conflicts and natural disasters.[6]

The Guiding Principles do not rise to the level of a binding treaty that nations are obligated to follow. It should be noted, however, that many of the rights mentioned in the Principles are binding on the United States because the same concepts appear in the binding ICCPR and ICERD treaties. Moreover, all countries, including the United States, are aware of the Principles and can look to them for direction when national conditions lead to internal upheavals in population. Furthermore, in 2005 the United Nations General Assembly stated that it recognized the Principles as an "important international framework for the protection of internally displaced people."[7] Finally, according to Francis Deng, the Principles "reflect and are consistent with international human rights and humanitarian law and analogous refugee law."[8]

Under Principle 1, internally displaced people are entitled to the full rights that all other persons in the country enjoy. The Principle does not limit itself to citizens, but applies to all persons. This is important because there were thousands of permanent residents, lawful temporary residents, and undocumented people in the areas affected by Hurricane Katrina. Undocumented immigrants were eligible for short-term disaster relief. Yet, the Department of Homeland Security made it clear that such people would have no immunity from deportation. Many were detained, and deportation proceedings were started against them. Also, while undocumented workers are not entitled to many benefits under U.S. law, they are entitled to send their children to school. Nonetheless, doing so may call their status to the attention of the authorities in the new communities where they settled.

Under Principle 3, it is the primary obligation of the national authorities to implement the rights afforded to internally displaced persons. While local authorities would certainly be involved, the ultimate responsibility in the United States would be on the federal level. It is clear that in the case of Hurricane Katrina, a disproportionate number of black people and poor people could not, and many still cannot, exercise those rights, because of government failures at the local, state, and federal levels.

According to Principle 4, certain groups are especially entitled to protection, including children, pregnant mothers, mothers with young children, female heads of households, persons with disabilities, and the elderly. Once again, it is evident that our government failed these specially protected groups. How many newborns died in the aftermath of the hurricane? How many pregnant women miscarried? We heard of the tragic story of a nursing home where the bodies of thirty-four elderly people were found, and cases where the elderly would not leave their homes and died as a result.[9]

The Guiding Principles are concerned with all aspects of dislocation: protection against displacement, protection while displaced, and protection after displacement. With respect to protection against displacement, Principle 7 makes clear that the authorities are supposed to provide proper accomodations with adequate safety, nutrition, health, and hygiene. The failure of the government to provide transportation to relocate people before the hurricane struck was one failure related to this Principle. Even days later when transportation was brought in, the people on the buses did not have proper food or water, nor were they told where they were going.

The horrors that took place in the New Orleans Convention Center and the Superdome also illustrate how government failed to live up to this Principle. Displaced people lacked food, water, bedding, and proper sanitation. Finally, when black people tried to obtain basic needs such as food and water that the government failed to provide to them, they were labeled as looters.

According to Principle 7, family members should not be separated. Yet, many family members remained separated for months after the hurricane, including large numbers of children.

Additionally, according to the Principles, displacement should not violate "the rights to life, dignity, liberty, and security." Nevertheless, many people died not as result of the hurricane, but after the levees were breached and the area was flooded. Cutting the budget of the Army Corps of Engineers, which could have protected against the breaching of the levees, must constitute a gross dereliction of the federal government's obligation to protect life. It was well known that the levees would be breached with a hurricane of this magnitude.

Under Principle 6, displacement should also not last longer than required. Yet, there are numerous examples of people waiting many months for FEMA trailers, which could provide temporary housing as they try to rebuild or repair their homes.

The second area that the Principles discuss concerns protection during displacement. Principle 10 protects the right to life. Under international law, this term does not concern abortion. Instead, it covers protection against murder and other related types of violence. Nonetheless, there may have been incidents in the convention center and the Superdome where the authorities were not in control of law and order, and people were attacked. Additionally, authorities dropping people off on highways for days without follow-up would constitute a violation of this principle of the right to life and security.

Internally displaced persons also have a right to dignity and physical and mental integrity (Principle 11). I remember the images of dead bodies lying for days in front of distraught and hungry black people. It is hard to imagine the nightmares that the children who witnessed such horrors are having. Are they getting psychotherapy or other proper medical treatment?

Under Principle 11, people should be protected against gender-specific violence, such as rape and assault. Yet, there were apparently various incidents of this kind, both inside and outside of the convention center and the Superdome.

Principle 16 is one of the most touching. Under that Principle, the displaced have a right to know the fate of missing relatives, and the state should collect and identify remains and return them to the next of kin. Months after the disaster, there are still many unclaimed remains and more than several thousand missing persons. DNA testing did not start as quickly as it should have. The media, rather than the government, have often taken the lead in locating missing persons and, sadly, helping to match survivors with remains of loved ones.

According to Principle 17, family members who want to remain together should be able to do so. Yet, that too has not happened.

Under Principle 18, displaced persons are also entitled to an adequate standard of living. The Principle quantifies this vague term by stating that, at a minimum, the authorities should provide access to food, shelter, water, housing, clothing, and health care. Of course, one of the ironies is that many of the displaced people did not have adequate access to these items even while they were living in their homes. Unlike most other developed nations, the United States does not recognize many of these economic, social, and cultural rights in its constitution.

Medical care is of special concern (Principle 19). The images of people wading though fetid, polluted waters come to mind. The number of evacuees who must have been exposed to contagious diseases and unclean conditions in the convention center and the Superdome must be great. Many people did not have the proper access to medication for treating their chronic conditions. Moving from place to place or continuing to live in crowded temporary housing cannot be conducive to appropriate medical care.

Additionally, many people must be experiencing mild to severe depression because they may have lost everything—including family members. Their psychological needs could be the most pressing, yet least likely to be treated. Of special concern would be the needs of the people who were mentally ill before the hurricane. Keeping them on their medications can be difficult in the best of circumstances. Some may have been homeless or living in group homes or with family members before the disaster. Being uprooted and lacking access to any medication or their disability income may have led to truly dangerous situations for themselves or others when they ended up in areas where no one knew them or their specific medical needs.

Principle 19 also mentions the special needs of women, including reproductive care and special counseling for victims of sexual abuse. In addition to the unfortunate situation of pregnant women mentioned above, a host of gynecological needs have probably been ignored in this period.

Principle 20 concerns the responsibility of the government to provide necessary documentation to displaced people. Various government buildings in New Orleans and other communities were damaged. A U.S. passport agency located in New Orleans was damaged as well. How many people have not been able to get the documents they need to start new lives? To start most jobs, one must show proof of work authorization: a U.S. birth certificate or passport or a foreign passport and work visa, for example. To rent an apartment, identification must be provided in most instances. Documents such as marriage licenses, voter cards, driver's licenses, birth and death certificates, and child support and divorce records could all be needed for people transitioning to new communities.

A very important principle concerns rights in property. Principle 21 states that no one should be arbitrarily deprived of property or possessions. It appears that landlords may have unceremoniously dumped their tenants' belongings on the street without attempting to find the tenants, in order to rent the apartments out for higher prices. Moreover, there is great fear that the city of New Orleans may bulldoze properties without giving proper notice.

Principle 22 states that there should be no discrimination in the right to vote or to participate in community and public affairs. Fall elections in New Orleans were postponed until the spring. Many are worried about the ability of evacuees to vote in person or by absentee ballot. How likely is it that the bankrupt city government will have the resources to run a proper election, especially with so many displaced residents, who would need absentee ballots? Many black residents fear that the city will "turn white" because they will not be able to vote for black leadership.

Principle 23 concerns the right to education. Ironically, many evacuees may get a better education now that they have abandoned the failed New Orleans school system. Louisiana schools are generally among the worst in the nation. On the other hand, problems have occurred in the Houston schools, as local students resent the New Orleans students. Given the degree of miseducation, how many of these New Orleans children will be neglected in classes where they are just too far behind their peers? How many teachers will mistake depression for stupidity and ignore them?

The final area that the Principles cover is protection after displacement: return, resettlement, and reintegration. Principle 28 requires the government to help establish the conditions necessary to allow displaced persons to either return to their areas of residence or be resettled voluntarily. The displaced themselves are supposed to participate in the planning and management of their return. Many people now forced to live outside the Big Easy are worried that they and their needs are being excluded from the redevelopment plans for the area. Many are still concerned with survival—solidifying a job, dealing with creditors, obtaining copies of documents, dealing with school problems, and obtaining more permanent housing for their families. Most are hundreds of miles away from New Orleans. They do not have the time or the ability to stay on top of what redevelopment plans are being considered by the power elite back home. How effectively have all levels of government helped all the evacuees keep in touch?

According to Principle 29, the displaced are not to be discriminated against in the provision of services, whether they return home or live elsewhere. Unfortunately, it appears that after an initial groundswell of sympathy in many places, the evacuees may have worn out their welcome rather quickly. Race, class, and cultural differences coupled with preexisting stereotypes have led to discrimination at many levels. Yet, many are trying to blend into new communities and start afresh. They do not plan to return to New Orleans, a place where they suffered from lack of educational and employment opportunities and stigmatization.

The authorities are also supposed to help the displaced recover their property and possessions. If this is not possible, the authorities must "provide or assist those persons in obtaining appropriate compensation or another form of just reparation" (Principle 29).

Many homeowners lost everything but did not have proper insurance coverage for flooding. Will the federal government make the insurance companies pay up anyway, or cover the losses from federal funds? If a bank foreclosed on a devastated property after the initial three-month hiatus on collecting mortgage payments, is the federal government stepping in to prevent that or to cover the payments? Naturally, many people were renters and lacked rental insurance that would cover this disaster. Will the government step in to replace their valuables or prevent them from being evicted or rent gouged?

The Guiding Principles provide a comprehensive framework for all levels of government in the United States still grappling with providing services in the aftermath of Hurricane Katrina. While the Principles are not binding on the United States, they certainly could aid our government in measuring our efforts under internationally agreed upon standards.

As a new hurricane season approaches with many megastorms expected, it is unfortunate that few officials are likely to have heard of these Principles, much less consulted them. In the future, relevant government officials need to be made more aware. How? The State Department and the United Nations representative are the federal entities most likely to be familiar with the Guiding Principles. These offices could distribute them to various federal agencies like FEMA. Then, follow-up would have to be done to make sure relevant officials understood the value of the Principles and would actually consult them as they revised their generic disaster-relief plans as well as region-specific plans. Moreover, human rights nongovernmental organizations like Amnesty International and Human Rights Watch, plus lawyers groups like Human Rights First, the American Society for International Law, the American

Bar Association, and the National Lawyers Guild, could all play a positive role. With sufficient media assistance, including use of the Internet, such groups could help educate government officials, disaster relief organizations such as the Red Cross, and the general public.

As a society, we must vigilantly monitor the long-term human-rights status and treatment of the Katrina victims wherever they may be located. As General Beauregard's great-great-granddaughter, I want to be part of the process of ensuring that the New Orleans black community as it was once constituted is not forgotten. National, state, and local governments must be made to live up to their various domestic *and* international legal obligations over the years to come. They should consult internationally derived documents like the Guiding Principles as well.

NOTES

This chapter draws on two presentations I have made on this topic. A panel on the aftermath of Katrina was held at the University of Iowa College of Law on September 22, 2005. I would like to thank the various student groups at Iowa, including the Black Law Student Association, who sponsored that event. Additionally, the Texas Southern University Thurgood Marshall School of Law held a conference entitled "Post Katrina: An Analysis of Federal, State and Local Governmental Challenges; Race, Class, Gender Issues; First Amendment and Media Controversies; Immigration and International Law Implications" on November 18, 2005. I would like to thank especially Professor Craig Jackson for inviting me to that event. Finally, I would like to thank my research assistants, Brendan Hug, Simba Hodari, Sam Sadden, and especially Ozan Varol.

1. UN Doc. E/CN.4/1998/53/Add. 2. For further discussion of the Prin-

ciples, see Frederic L. Kirgis, "Victims of Hurricane Katrina Are Internally Displaced Persons, not Refugees," *American Society of International Law Insight,* September 21, 2005, www.asil.org/insights/2005/09/insights050921.html.

2. The ICCPR was adopted in 1966 and entered into force in 1976. The United States ratified it in 1992. The text can be found at www.ohchr.org/english/law/ccpr.htm. The ICERD was adopted in 1965 and entered into force in 1969. The United States ratified it in October 1994. The text can be found at www.ohchr.org/english/law/cerd.htm.

3. The text of the ICESCR can be found at www.ohchr.org/english/law/cescr.htm. The text of the CRC can be found at www.ohchr/english/crc/htm. The text of the CEDAW can be found at http://www.ohchr/english/cedaw.htm.

4. For a discussion of the various human rights violations by the U.S. government, see "Statement of Jeanne Woods and Hope Lewis Prepared for the Hearings of the United Nations Special Rapporteur on Extreme Poverty on the Aftermath of Hurricane Katrina," October 27, 2005, www.slaw.neu.edu/clinics/WoodsLewis.pdf; the National Lawyers Guild, "Resolution on U.S. Government Violations of Human Rights of Katrina Victims," October 29, 2005, www.mcli.org/reso-nlg-katrina2-4pdf.pdf. For further discussion, see also the proceedings from the Texas Southern University Thurgood Marshall School of Law conference entitled "Post Katrina: An Analysis of Federal, State and Local Governmental Challenges; Race, Class, Gender Issues; First Amendment and Media Controversies; Immigration and International Law Implications," held on November 18, 2005. Many of the papers from this conference are published in the *Texas Southern University Law Review.* Professor George E. Edwards presented a paper entitled "International Human Rights Law Violations Pre-, During and Post-Hurricane Katrina: An International Law Framework for Analysis." If this paper has not been published in the *Texas*

Southern University Law Review, then contact Professor Edwards directly, gedwards@indiana.edu, for its location.

5. The convention was adopted on July 28, 1951. There is a 1967 protocol as well. There are also regional documents such as the 1969 Refugee Convention of the Organization of American States.

6. Foreword to second edition of the Guiding Principles on Internal Displacement by Undersecretary General for Humanitarian Affairs and Emergency Relief Coordinator Mr. Jan Egeland, September 2004.

7. See www.un.org/summit2005/Draft_Outcome130905.pdf.

8. Introductory Note to the Guiding Principles by Mr. Francis M. Deng.

9. See "Nursing Home Owners Face Charges," *CNN.com,* September 13, 2005, www.cnn.com/2005/US/09/13/katrina.impact/(last visited January 30, 2006).

10.

THE STATION
Anthony Paul Farley

*Our age is on the eve of a revolt against property, in the name of the
common claim of all to a common share in the results of the common
labour of all.[1]*
—Charlotte Wilson, "Freedom"

but this is your hour, and the power of darkness.[2]
—Luke 22:53

The train has already left the station. The shadows within are waiting for nothing. The station is the zero point of white power. Progress is measured by how long the train's been gone. The lines all lead toward white power.

Railways are built on high ground. Whiteness is wealth and wealth lives above sea level in New Orleans. Poverty casts its black shadows into the depths. The flood was no accident. As the psychoanalysts so often repeat, there are no accidents. The unrepaired levee was the instrument by which the whites dispossessed the blacks of the depths and cast them into yet deeper waters.

On August 27, 2005, the last Amtrak train left the station filled with equipment but without any passengers. On the twenty-eighth, evacuation was made mandatory. On the twenty-ninth, the levee was breached. On September 11, in the *Washington Post* and on NBC's *Meet the Press,* the mayor and Amtrak would each deny responsibility for the *last* empty train. The last train, of course, hardly mattered in the overall tragic scene. Why trains, plural and modern and fast, were not running around the clock to evacuate everyone remains an unasked, and unanswered, question. Not until October 9, when a train called the City of New Orleans pulled into the station, was railway service restored to New Orleans, and the return of railway service is not an answer to the question of why service was ended when it was needed to save lives.

In New Orleans, the color line separates the drowned from the saved, and that line was laid a long time ago. Amtrak could have been used to save people from the flood. It was not. That decision was also made a long time ago. To understand why the railway was not used, and why the levee was allowed to break, and the market for the horrifying spectacle that followed, one must travel backward in time.

New Orleans was a slave market. Black was the mark used to differentiate owners from owned. The blacks were for sale. The mark was a pleasure and a passion. It was such a pleasure that it kept coming undone. Hierarchy based on racial marking expressed itself as rape and then as the reproductive undoing of the already-fictional biology of racial difference that kept white over black. Hierarchy expressed itself as rape and forced reproduction, and forced reproduction meant whites who were not so white and blacks who were not so black. All of which fueled the passion for racial marking all the more. This passion was the market.

The owner owns in order to be an owner. Ownership is an experience of the flesh; it enters the flesh through the mark. Ownership, then, is pleasure and can be felt only through the pain of the dispossessed, and the pain of dispossession can be felt only through the pleasure of the owner. These are pleasures and pains of comparison. The suffering and surrender of the dispossessed is necessary for the owner to experience the pleasure of ownership. Ownership, moreover, is addictive. Where the pleasure of ownership expressed itself through rape and forced reproduction, the children of this dispossession were sold as slaves on a specialized market, one for racially indeterminate sex slaves, centered in New Orleans.

Modern progress measured itself station by station and rail by rail as new lands and new peoples, new accumulations, were ever more speedily brought to the market. The market expanded as it ever more speedily gathered everything into itself. The expansion of the market was the forward progress of the owners. The locomotive thus arrived in the world as a thing of beauty and a joy forever, but not to everyone and not everywhere.

The railway splits the land, and white worms, monstrous from their feast, crawl out of this fatal injury to the commons. The parasites lay hold of the entire world. Middle Passage and Manifest Destiny, Infinite Justice and Enduring Freedom; this is the way the world ends, with the division of the commons and the marking of bodies for ownership and dispossession.

I use the metaphor of the railway to show the way that race and class were both put in place, like parallel rails, for the same purpose, to carry the white owners across the land and into the future. I use the metaphor of the station to show the futility of waiting. I use the psychoanalytic concepts of "trauma" and "screen memory" to describe why black people continue to turn to the law even though the law has never led them anywhere. I use the idea of "free association" to show a way for black consciousness to cease its repetitive return to the legal tracks and instead turn to mutual aid and direct action.

The conflict over space—over what is to become of the city of New Orleans—obscures the conflict over time. Ownership divides space into *mine* or *yours* or *his* or *hers* or *theirs* or *ours*. The division that gives rise to the property relation must first be made on the flesh. Property must be written on the body because before we are divided into *haves* and *have-nots* we are all, equally, held by and holders of the skin we are in. Without the marking of bodies there can be no division into owners and dispossessed. At the level of economy, the relation between owner and dispossessed is parasitic; the former is the parasite of the latter. The inaugural mark of our system of property relations was written on black flesh with steel chains. The chains marked and continue to mark the division of the body into white over black. The marks laid down in white over black, once set in place, continue forever into the future like rails to infinity; the train can travel only to the station.

Whites own the areas above sea level in New Orleans. Owners always want more, so the dispossessions, once they begin, continue parasitically until the host is dead. Whites need to take continually from blacks. Owners transform all of nature into property, that is, into a means for further dispossession. Congressman Richard Baker seemed to celebrate the loss of black life as the miracle of white wealth. In his own words, "We finally cleaned up public housing in New Orleans. We couldn't do it, but God did." Unoccupied housing is still empty in dry areas of New Orleans. The whites are returning and blacks are still being kept out. Plans have already been presented to transform black areas of the city's Lower Ninth Ward into water-retention plains to protect white, wealthier areas.

There were no race relations before the violence of accumulation; the violence of ownership gives us our first sense of the otherwise quite unremarkable—because unfetishized—difference in the color of the skin we are in. Ownership does something else as well. Ownership also makes us forget that things were not always this way. This is something it accomplishes by creating a time out of mind, a memory of humankind that runs only on the rails of capitalist necessity and no others. Ownership is also the conquest of time.

"God gave Noah the rainbow sign. No more water, the fire next time!"[3] Time, like space, is *theirs* or *ours*. Time, the slaves perceived, through the crystal of their dispossession, is white over black. The genealogy of any object of property leads back to an original accumulation. The legal system is a collection of these genealogies. The original accumulation, the violent capture of peoples and lands that must take place in order for there to be property, appears within the legal system as a time out of mind. To seek the future through legal means is to bow down before a certain tradition "of higher antiquity than memory or history can reach; nothing being more difficult than to ascertain the precise beginning and first spring of an ancient and long established custom." This tradition, the unwritten law or *lex non scripta* of the kingdom, the common law, the foundation of our law, has been in place for "time out of mind; or, in the solemnity of our legal phrase, time whereof the memory of man runneth not to the contrary."[4] The Middle Passage and Manifest Destiny, the original accumulation that provides the owners' initial capital, belong to that time out of mind. The common law, the foundation of our law, then, comes to us from the time out of mind of the original dispossession.

Master and slave have nothing in common, other than the chains that bind. The parasitic or capitalist relation of the former to the latter is born of the division of the commons. The space of the master and the space of the slave are mutually exclusive. The time of the master cannot be the time of the slave. Space and time belong to the owner. Law and property perpetually remind the slave who owns what. Law and property also make the slave forget what time it is. The two processes—memory and forgetting—are related and can be observed in the slaves' search for lost time.

New Orleans is one of the oldest places in the New World. We live our childhood as our future. As with the individual, so with the collective, and so the tale of the city can be told as the tale of the child who grows up but never crosses the horizon of a traumatic event—a traumatic event that is never really over because it was never really understood. The trauma of the original accumulation, of slavery, is such a trauma. The white-over-black relationship, laid down in law and property, is parasitic and was so from the beginning, when the tracks were laid. Those tracks lead only in the direction of white over black, like rails to infinity. No help was ever coming to save the blacks from the flood. The levee broke long before any of the victims were born.

Property is a very curious thing:

> Property—not the claim to use, but a right to prevent others from using—enables individuals who have appropriated the means of production, to hold in subjection all those who possess nothing but their vital energy, and who must work that they may live.[5]

Every object of property has a genealogy. The average black child today is born into a family with no net financial assets. Within the system of property, the legal system, then, she is an orphan. It could not be otherwise; she was orphaned before conception, she was orphaned by the original accumulation. When the black child, the child with nothing of her own, traces the genealogy of her dispossession, of her lost time, she finds nothing. It is as if she never existed. The black child was never meant to exist; that is the meaning of the racial mark, white over black, of the original accumulation. The search for lost time begins and ends in the station. Such abandonment is too much to be borne, too much to take. Abandonment is traumatic and therefore remembered only in the form of a screen memory, a scene that unfolds within a peculiar time outside of mind, and repeats. Such abandonment is what we saw unfold in the televised spectacle of blacks on rooftops hoping for helicopters that never stopped.

Our childhoods, say the psychoanalysts, remain with us complete and entire. Unbearable thoughts and feelings—and the memories associated with them—cannot be undone, but they can be forced underground. The unconscious is the space of such banished memories. Psychoanalytically, then, to "forget" early experiences or scenes is to repress them, to force them underground. Sometimes what actually took place is hidden (covered over or screened) by a replacement memory of a scene that never took place. Such screen memories themselves sometimes determine our future actions. These screen memories get hold of us with all the force of the original trauma, and thus we move backward into the future. The picture, the screen memory, seems to get hold of the mind in a peculiar way: "The patient does not remember anything of what he has forgotten and repressed, but acts it out. He reproduces it not as a memory but as an action; he repeats it, without, of course, knowing that he is repeating it."⁶ The more unbearable the memory, the greater the resistance, and "[t]he greater the resistance, the more extensively will acting out (repetition) replace remembering."[7]

Black fidelity to law—witness the endless and fruitless search for equal rights and justice of "this species of property"—has to do with the hold of just such a peculiar screen memory. Black resistance to the memory of slavery takes the form of fidelity to the dream of equal rights and justice under law and, therefore, to the repetition of the original accumulation. "The first step in overcoming the resistances is made, as we know, by the analyst's uncovering the resistance, which is never recognized by the patient, and acquainting him with it."[8]

Sometimes, sitting on a train as it slides through space, just behind the wall of sleep, there is a moment when everything falls away and one enters the time of the dream. In the time of the dream, it seems as if all things are possible, as if we can go home again. It is within the space of just such an "as if" that the black struggle for equal rights and justice takes place.

The black railway journey toward rights is a result of a picture, a scene, a screen memory, having got hold. The scene never took place. The scene is a screen memory; it hides the unbearable fact of the original accumulation. The Founding Fathers at the end of the line are the ones who instituted white over black; it is, therefore, not possible for the object of property to meet the Founding Fathers in the Promised Land. The object of property was made an object of property by the white slave master at the zero point of the very genealogy that it searches; it is therefore in search of lost time. The black experience of the railway is not only a metaphor; it runs through the black experience of the Jim Crow South and to the legal tracks laid down by Homer Plessy.

Homer Plessy, one-eighth black and by all appearances white, and thus literally embodying all the contradictions of the mark, was arrested in 1892 for violating the law mandating separate railway carriages for whites and blacks. In the landmark case *Plessy v. Ferguson,* Justice Henry Brown wrote for the majority and upheld "separate but equal," citing *Roberts v. City of Boston,* an 1849 school segregation case.[9] Justice John Marshall Harlan, dissenting on the segregation point, agreed with the broader principle of white over black:

> The white race deems itself to be the dominant race in this country. And so it is, in prestige, in achievements, in education, in wealth, and in power. So, I doubt not, it will continue to be *for all time,* if it remains true to its great heritage, and holds fast to the principles of constitutional liberty.[10]

For the *Plessy* majority *and* for the dissent, for white supporters and white opponents of segregation, white over black was to continue, as a certainty, "for all time." Win or lose, *Brown v. Board I* and *Brown v. Board II,* every outcome of the quest for rights was to end in white over black, "for all time." Fifty plus years after *Brown v. Board* turned Harlan's dissent into the law of the land, the schools are still segregated. The black quest for rights, the search for lost time, begins and ends at the station. That is the meaning of "for all time." The legal routes were all laid down, like rails to infinity, at the original accumulation.

When the levee broke, it was only as accidental as the original accumulation. When Amtrak was not used to save black souls from the rising waters of the flood, it was only as accidental as the original accumulation. There are no accidents. Every accident is an accumulation that has already taken place. Hurricane Katrina did not bring the first flood to New Orleans. Every natural disaster strikes with the force of the original accumulation, that is, the slavery that predetermines, even prophesies, who will be drowned and who will be saved. All of these tragedies are fixed by the original dispossession in which who is to own and who is to be property is designated by a mark on the flesh, by white over black.

The screen memory that animates the black quest for equal rights and justice, the wait at the station, is of a kindly Founding Father welcoming them to the Promised Land. But blacks were *abandoned* in the station. There are no Founding Fathers for the blacks; at the end of the line, there are only slave masters, white owners, whose many mansions can all be traced back to the original dispossession. The picture of the Founding Fathers that animates the black quest for rights is, more or less, like this: "the rights of all, as they are settled and regulated by law, are equally entitled to the *paternal consideration* and protection of the law, for maintenance and security." [11]

That the portrait of the Founding Fathers' "paternal consideration" is a screen memory (screening the unbearable, traumatic memory of slavery) that has got hold of the blacks who endlessly and unconsciously refer to it in their legislative and litigative searches for lost time can be seen in the fact that the words just quoted are from *Roberts v. City of Boston,* the case cited in *Plessy* for the principle of "separate but equal."

Revisiting the trauma, that is, seeing the "paternal consideration" of the Founding Fathers as the screen memory it is, is difficult, but "[o]ne must allow the patient time to become more conversant with this resistance with which he has now become acquainted, to work through it, to overcome it, by continuing, in defiance of it, the analytic work according to the fundamental rule of analysis." [12] And it takes time, which means that time must be taken or seized. The "fundamental rule" of psychoanalysis is free association.

The group has a problem, the "black problem." The blacks are a group, not an individual; the free associations, accordingly, are to be found in the relations that individuals within the group form with each other. Their relations, forms of black interaction, reveal the trauma. Dispossession is traumatic. When the slaves are marked for slavery they are dispossessed of everything; it is the end of their world and the beginning of their master's world. Their flesh is marked as property, and because property cannot own property, the slaves can own nothing, not even the skin they are in. The violence of this dispossession is too great to be borne; the bodies and minds made to bear this unbearable violence are split apart, white over black. The patients have a symptom, the blacks wait for already-departed trains and progress, that is the way their trauma has frozen, so to speak, in the form of a symptom: the blacks wait at the station. White progress, on the other hand, is measured by how long the train's been gone. New Orleans figures in the history of the slave market and in the slave's post-Emancipation search for lost time. The train, Plessy's, seems much like the unused Amtrak line, and the flood is the major sign of the end of one era and the beginning of another, and that is what we think we want, a new era, by water or by fire. Because we repeatedly look down the tracks of law and property, waiting for a Founding Father to welcome us to the Promised Land of equal rights and justice, our struggles, on all the territories crossed by the rails, become their time. Our struggles become white time because they will always win. They will always win because the rails lead only to the station. Our eternal wait is what makes the time seem so very long.

We might do well, then, to look at the free associations made during the flood. Free associations of blacks gathered to take food and water from stores and distribute them to those who were thirsty and hungry. These associations were not for profit, nor were they forced; they were free. The distribution of the goods expropriated from the owners was according to need, a need each individual was left free to assess on her own. The flood opened an opportunity for the healthy operation of the instinct for mutual aid. Direct action, as the Wobblies used to say, gets the goods. Some, not all, but enough, began working out new forms of cooperation and direct action to provide examples of a new time, began doing something that constituted a strike, not yet general, against the spectacle, and, more important, began working through the trauma of the original accumulation.

New forms, examples of what free associations can do to seize the time by taking direct action and working out diverse embodiments of the instinct for mutual aid, emerged from the floodwaters of New Orleans. Not many, but some examples, and even the smallest mustard seed . . . enough to seize the time. As the blacks who took direct action by expropriating and redistributing needed water and food demonstrated in New Orleans, another world is possible. It is possible to break this timeline. It is possible to turn away from the altar of self-sacrifice that is the station and by mutual aid end the repetition of the primal scene of accumulation. Undoing the original accumulation, white over black, requires the end of law and of property and the unraveling of this time altogether. The new beginning is somewhere after the General Strike, but total and accomplishable by those who have only their empty hands.

NOTES

I thank David Dante Troutt for his editorial comments and for conceiving of this important and timely project. I thank Whitney Rivera and John Terpin for their wonderful research assistance. I thank Maria Grahn-Farley for her love and advice.

1. Charlotte Wilson, "Freedom," in *Anarchist Essays* 57, 58 (Nicolas Walter ed., Freedom Press: 2000) (1886).

2. Luke 22:53 (King James version).

3. Slave spiritual, quoted in James Baldwin, *The Fire Next Time* (1963).

4. *Blackstone's Commentary on the Laws of England,* book 1, section 1.

5. Charlotte Wilson, "Freedom," in *Anarchist Essays* 57, 58 (Nicolas Walter ed., Freedom Press: 2000), (1886). Wilson continues, "No work is possible without land, materials, and tools or machinery; thus the masters of these things are masters also of destitute workers, and can live in idleness upon their labour, paying them in wages only enough of the produce to keep them alive, only employing so many of them as they find profitable and leaving the rest to their fate. Such a wrong once realized is not to be borne." Ibid.

6. Sigmund Freud, "Remembering, Repeating and Working Through," in *The Standard Edition of the Complete Psychological Works of Sigmund Freud* (translated from the German under the general editorship of James Strachey in collaboration with Anna Freud, assisted by Alix Strachey and Alan Tyson); 24 vols. (London: Hogarth, 1953–74), vol. 12, 150.

7. Ibid.

8. Ibid.

9. *Plessy v. Ferguson,* 163 U.S. 537 (1896) (citing *Roberts v. City of Boston,* 59 Mass. [5 Cush.] 198, 206 [1850]).

10. *Plessy v. Ferguson,* 163 U.S. 537, 559 (1896) (Harlan, J., dissenting) (italics added).

11. *Roberts v. City of Boston,* 59 Mass. (5 Cush.) 198, 206 (1850).

12. Freud, "Remembering, Repeating and Working Through."

Derrick Bell has had a forty-eight-year career as a civil rights litigator, an administrator, a teacher, a writer, and a lecturer. He is the author of ten books, including *Race, Racism, and American Law* (5th edition, 2004), *Faces at the Bottom of the Well* (Basic Books, 1992), and *Silent Covenants:* Brown v. Board of Education *and the Unfilled Promise of Racial Justice* (Oxford University Press, 2004). Professor Bell is a visiting professor at New York University Law School.

Devon W. Carbado is professor of law at the UCLA School of Law, where he teaches constitutional law, constitutional criminal procedure, and critical race theory. His writings appear in law reviews at Michigan, Yale, UCLA, and Harvard, among other places. He has edited three books; his most recent, *Time on Two Crosses: The Collected Writings of Bayard Rustin* (with Don Weise), won a Lambda Literary Award.

Sheryll Cashin, professor of law at Georgetown University, writes about race relations, government, and inequality in America. Her recent book, *The Failures of Integration: How Race and Class are Undermining the American Dream* (Public Affairs, 2004) received critical praise in the *New York Times Book Review* among other publications. Cashin worked in the Clinton White House as an adviser on urban and economic policy and was law clerk to Supreme Court Justice Thurgood Marshall.

Michael Eric Dyson, named one of the one hundred most influential African Americans by *Ebony,* is a professor of humanities, religious studies, and Africana studies at the University of Pennsylvania, and author of more than twelve books, including *Come Hell or High Water: Hurricane Katrina and the Color of Disaster* (Basic Civitas, 2006).

Anthony Paul Farley is associate professor of law at the Boston College Law School. He received his J.D. from Harvard Law School. His work is in constitutional law and legal theory.

Cheryl I. Harris, professor of law at the UCLA School of Law, teaches in the areas of constitutional law, civil rights, critical race theory, and employment discrimination. Her publications include the groundbreaking "Whiteness as Property" *(Harvard Law Review),* as well as other major works in critical race theory. In 2003 she was a fellow at the University of California Humanities Research Institute, focusing on issues of redress, and in 2005 she received the Distinguished Professor for Civil Rights Education Award from the ACLU Foundation of Southern California.

Professor Charles J. Ogletree Jr. is the Jesse Climenko Professor of Law, and the founder and executive director of the Charles Hamilton Houston Institute for Race and Justice at Harvard Law School. He is the author of *All Deliberate Speed: Reflections on the First Half-Century of* Brown v. Board of Education (W. W. Norton, 2004) and F*rom Lynch Mobs to the Killing State: Race and the Death Penalty in America* (New York University Press, 2006).

Clement Alexander Price is Board of Governors Distinguished Service Professor of History and director of the Institute on Ethnicity, Culture, and the Modern Experience at Rutgers University. He is an authority on African American history, American urban history, and American public history. His publications include *Freedom Not Far Distant: a Documentary History of Afro-Americans in New Jersey* (New Jersey Historical Society, 1980) and *Many Voices, Many Opportunities: Cultural Pluralism and American Arts Policy* (Americans for the Arts, 1994).

Adolph L. Reed Jr. is a professor of political science at the University of Pennsylvania and a member of the interim council of the Labor Party.

Katheryn Russell-Brown is a professor of law and director of the Center for the Study of Race and Race Relations at the University of Florida, Levin College of Law. Professor Russell-Brown is the author of three books: *The Color of Crime* (New York University Press, 1998), *Underground Codes: Race, Crime, and Related Fires* (New York University Press, 2004), and *Protecting Our Own: Race, Crime, and African Americans* (Rowman & Littlefield, 2006). Dr. Russell-Brown's research, writing, and teaching have been in the areas of criminal law, sociology of law, and race and crime.

David Dante Troutt, professor of law and Justice John J. Francis Scholar at Rutgers Law School (Newark), teaches and writes on the law and theory of American ghettoes, race and critical theory, and intellectual property law. A former columnist and contributor to several national publications and essay anthologies, Professor Troutt authored *The Monkey Suit: Short Fiction on African Americans and Justice* for The New Press in 1998. His novel, *The Trouble Without You,* is forthcoming from Amistad.

John Valery White is J. Dawson Gasquet Memorial Professor of Law, Louisiana State University Law Center. A Louisiana native, Professor White is a Yale Law School graduate (1991) and former Schell Fellow at Human Rights Watch. He has taught at LSU since 1992, specializing in civil rights law and enforcement. His current work focuses on the effect of globalization-influenced migration on conceptions of civil and human rights.

Adrien Katherine Wing is the Bessie Dutton Murray Distinguished Professor of Law at the University of Iowa College of Law, where she has taught since 1987. She is also the associate dean for faculty development and research. Author of nearly eight publications, she is editor of *Critical Race Feminism* and *Global Critical Race Feminism.* She teaches critical race theory, U.S. constitutional law, and international law subjects.